Mapping *The* Cultures of the West

✳ ✳ ✳

Mapping
The Cultures
of the West

VOLUME 2: *since* 1350

CLIFFORD R. BACKMAN
Boston University

New York   Oxford
OXFORD UNIVERSITY PRESS

Oxford University Press is a department of the University of Oxford.
It furthers the University's objective of excellence in research,
scholarship, and education by publishing worldwide.

Oxford New York
Auckland Cape Town Dar es Salaam Hong Kong Karachi
Kuala Lumpur Madrid Melbourne Mexico City Nairobi
New Delhi Shanghai Taipei Toronto

With offices in
Argentina Austria Brazil Chile Czech Republic France Greece
Guatemala Hungary Italy Japan Poland Portugal Singapore
South Korea Switzerland Thailand Turkey Ukraine Vietnam

For titles covered by Section 112 of the US Higher Education
Opportunity Act, please visit www.oup.com/us/he for the
latest information about pricing and alternate formats.

Published by Oxford University Press
198 Madison Avenue, New York, New York 10016
http://www.oup.com

ISBN 978-0-19-997348-4

9 8 7 6

Printed in the United States of America
on acid-free paper

Contents

Contents vii

Outline Maps

Introduction

THERE ARE MANY WAYS TO TELL A STORY. Textbooks offer narratives, crafted by a modern historian or team of historians. Collections of primary sources present a mosaic of stories, often interspersed with pictures of artwork and other physical objects, drawn from the past. This sort of mosaic allows readers to take a more active role in constructing an overarching story—they recreate something of the process professional historians use to construct their narratives. Narratives and sourcebooks are often excellent at conveying political, social, and cultural developments in particular societies, partly because almost all sources, written or visual (or even archaeological), come from single societies, with travel narratives forming a rare and valuable exception.

This book takes a different approach to telling a story about Western civilization: it presents the West through a series of maps. Maps are not necessarily a better or worse medium for telling a global story. They are simply a different way, a way with its own advantages and disadvantages. Maps usually convey much less detail about the political and cultural details of particular societies than narratives and primary sources can. In addition, maps that adopt a "single-society" approach—the traditional sort of map of a politically defined country's political boundaries and centers of power—sometimes don't add much. They not only reinforce the sort of "nationalist" perspective narratives can lead to but can give a false sense of the independence, coherence, and isolation of such entities.

This book takes advantage of the strengths of maps to tell a different sort of story. Maps can reveal connections by tracing the network connections—of trade, migration, and cultural exchange—and geographic contexts of individual societies. This is valuable because the tension between individual societies, often defined politically, and broader networks, defined economically, socially, and culturally, is arguably one of the central dynamics of world historical development. Maps can also act as snapshots of social history, conveying in dramatic visual terms the aggregate social developments related to demographic and economic growth or change. Like the activities of networks, such deep social trends often do not show up clearly in political narratives or the literary sources generated by social elites. Maps can thus uncover neglected layers of social history. Finally, maps are perhaps the best medium for conveying the trans-regional and even global nature of many such deep processes, from the early emergence of networks of trade through the effect of industrialization on world-wide communications to the impact of global warming on the entire planet.

So, welcome to a story of Western civilization through maps—not a replacement for other stories, but a complementary look, another perspective on a story too vast and rich to be told in just one way.

Mapping *The* Cultures of the West

✳ ✳ ✳

29. Europe

1350–1453

✳ ✳ ✳

In 1328 Philip of Valois was able to assume the French crown by rights of descent through the male line, but he was challenged by Edward III of England, descended more directly from the last Capetians through his mother. The resulting war, an intermittent series of conflicts, was as much a French civil war as an Anglo-French contest. By 1453 the English had been expelled from all of France except Calais.

THE HUNDRED YEARS WAR 1337–1453

- Plantagenet territory c. 1300
- Plantagenet territory recognized by the Treaty of Brétigny 1360
- Area recognizing Plantagenet kingship 1420–28
- ✗ Major battle with date

The initial cause of the Great Schism was a disputed papal election in 1378. It lasted for almost forty years (1378–1417) because lay political groups exploited the situation, rapidly aligning themselves behind the rival claimants to papal office.

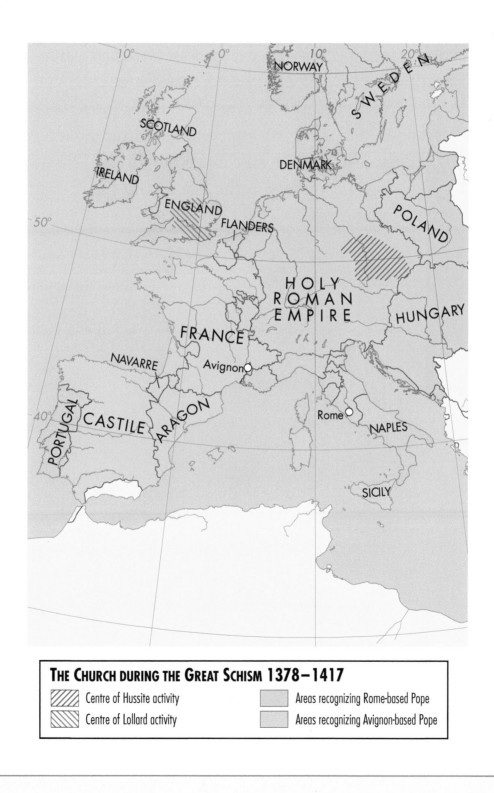

THE CHURCH DURING THE GREAT SCHISM 1378–1417

Centre of Hussite activity	Areas recognizing Rome-based Pope
Centre of Lollard activity	Areas recognizing Avignon-based Pope

30. The European Economy in the 15th Century

✳ ✳ ✳

Between about 1370 and 1500 the rural world was marked by depressed grain prices, partly offset by increasing diversification from arable into pasture farming and horticulture. With the contraction of the labor force, wages rose and sustained the demand for a wide range of manufactured and other commodities, both staples and luxuries. The result was a more buoyant economy in the towns and the fostering of technological innovation.

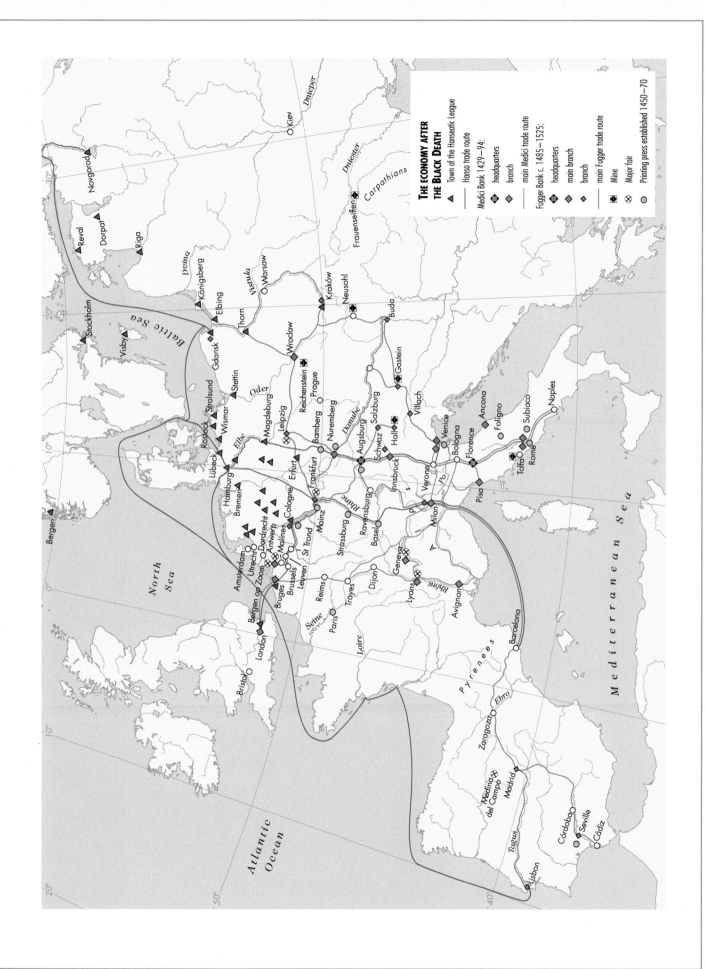

THE ECONOMY AFTER THE BLACK DEATH

▲ Town of the Hanseatic League

— Hansa trade route

Medici Bank 1429–94:
◆ headquarters
◆ branch
— main Medici trade route

Fugger Bank c. 1485–1525:
◆ headquarters
◆ main branch
◆ branch
— main Fugger trade route

✦ Mine
⊗ Major fair
○ Printing press established 1450–70

Novgorod

Reval
Dorpat
Riga

Kiev

Dniester

Dnieper

Carpathians

Frauenseiffen

Stockholm
Visby

Baltic Sea

Königsberg
Elbing
Thorn
Warsaw
Vistula
Dvina

Kraków
Neusohl
Buda

Gdansk
Stettin
Oder
Magdeburg
Leipzig
Wroclaw
Reichenstein
Prague
Gastein

Stralsund
Rostock
Wismar
Elbe
Bamberg
Nuremberg
Danube
Salzburg
Villach
Ancona

Lübeck
Hamburg
Erfurt
Frankfurt
Augsburg
Schwaz
Hall
Innsbruck
Venice
Bologna
Florence
Foligno
Subiaco
Naples

Bergen

North Sea

Bremen
Cologne
Mainz
Strassburg
Ravensburg
Basel
Alps
Verona
Milan
Po
Pisa
Tolfa
Rome

Amsterdam
Utrecht
Dordrecht
Antwerp
Malines
St Trond
Leuven
Brussels
Bruges
Bergen op Zoom
London
Bristol

Rhine
Reims
Troyes
Dijon
Geneva
Lyons
Rhône
Avignon

Seine
Paris
Loire

Pyrenees
Barcelona
Ebro
Zaragoza

Medina del Campo
Madrid

Atlantic Ocean

Tagus
Lisbon
Córdoba
Seville
Cádiz

Mediterranean Sea

31. The European Discovery of the World

1450–1600

✳ ✳ ✳

When Christopher Columbus set sail across the Atlantic in 1492, he was guided by the assertion that the circumference of the Earth was about 7000 miles shorter than

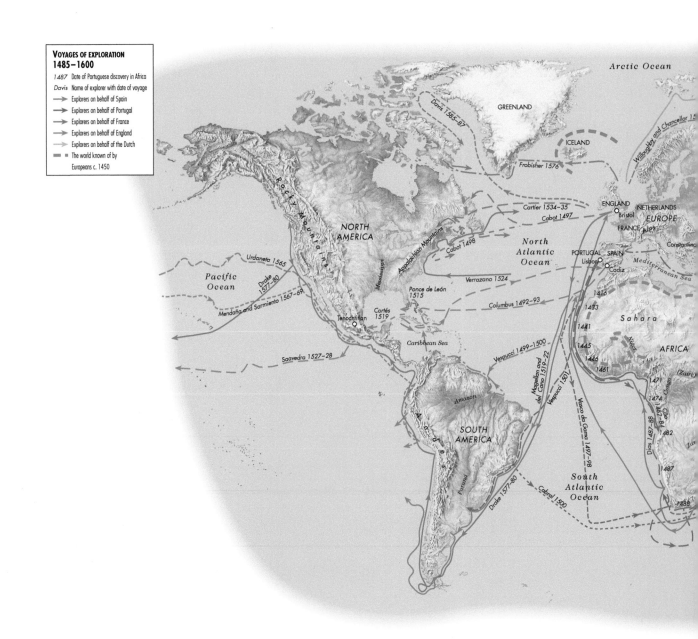

VOYAGES OF EXPLORATION
1485–1600

1487 Date of Portuguese discovery in Africa
Davis Name of explorer with date of voyage
→ Explorers on behalf of Spain
→ Explorers on behalf of Portugal
→ Explorers on behalf of France
→ Explorers on behalf of England
→ Explorers on behalf of the Dutch
– – ■ The world known of by Europeans c. 1450

Arctic Ocean

GREENLAND

ICELAND

Davis 1585–87

Willoughby and Chancellor 1553

Frobisher 1576

Cartier 1534–35

Cabot 1497

ENGLAND
Bristol
NETHERLANDS
EUROPE
FRANCE
PORTUGAL SPAIN
Lisbon
Cadiz
Constantino
Mediterranean Sea

Cabot 1498

North Atlantic Ocean

ROCKY Mountains

NORTH AMERICA

Appalachian Mountains

Mississippi

Verrazano 1524

Columbus 1492–93

Urdaneta 1565

Pacific Ocean

Drake 1577–80

Mendaña and Sarmiento 1567–69

Saavedra 1527–28

Ponce de León 1515

Cortés 1519

Tenochtitlan

Caribbean Sea

Vespucci 1499–1500

Magellan and del Cano 1519–22

Vespucci 1501

Vasco da Gama 1497–98

1416

1433

1441

1445

1446

1461

Sahara

AFRICA

1471

1474

1482–88

1482

1487

Amazon

SOUTH AMERICA

Andes

Paraná

Drake 1577–80

Cabral 1500

South Atlantic Ocean

Dias 1487–88

1486

it actually was. His belief that the West Indies were islands off the coast of China was quickly discredited when Spanish expeditions began to explore the Americas and, beyond them, the Pacific Ocean.

32. Europeans in Asia

1500–1750

✳ ✳ ✳

The Portuguese seaborne empire was based on a series of forts linking together trading entrepots from the coast of Africa to South and Southeast Asia and on to China and Japan. This system secured Portuguese trade with the East for nearly a century. The Europeans were drawn toward Asia by the lure of exotic consumer goods—tea, spices, and silk—and by high-quality manufactured goods such as porcelain and printed cotton textiles.

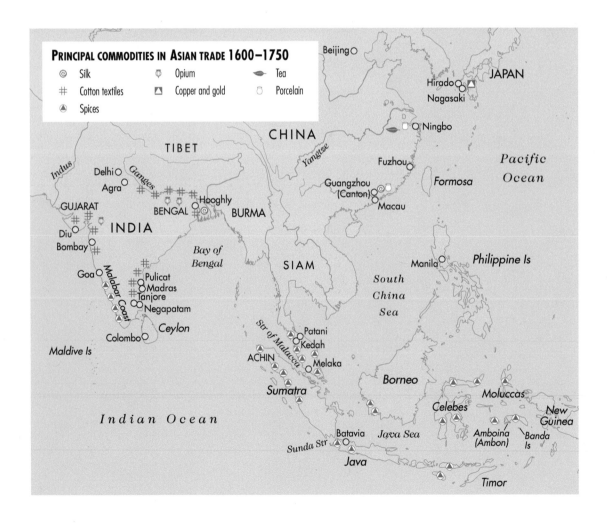

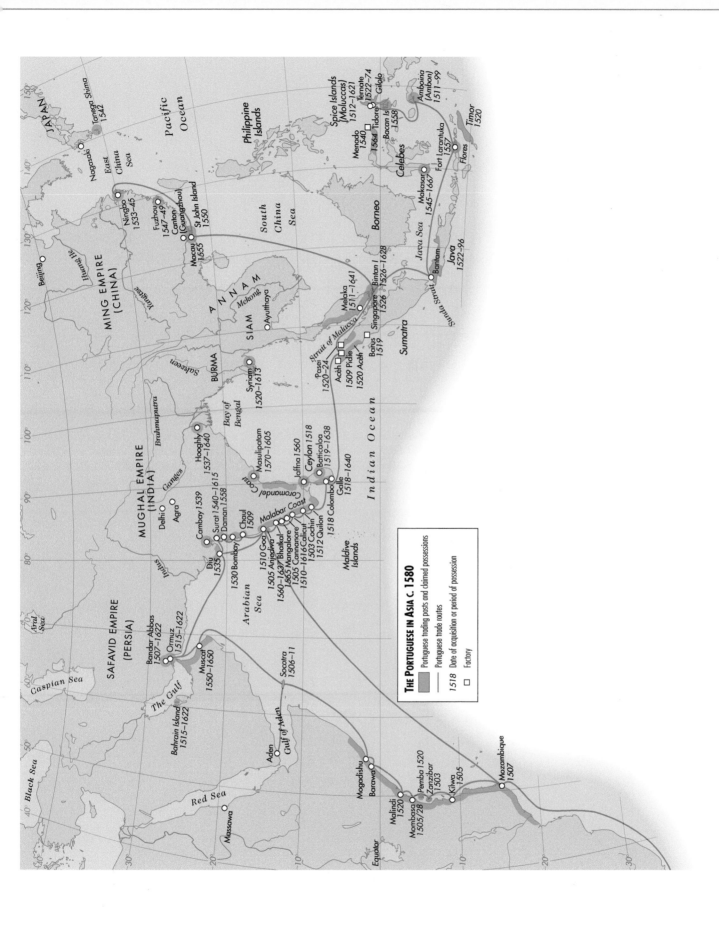

THE PORTUGUESE IN ASIA c. 1580

- Portuguese trading posts and claimed possessions
- —— Portuguese trade routes
- 1518 Date of acquisition or period of possession
- □ Factory

JAPAN

Nagasaki
Tanega Shima 1542

Pacific Ocean

East China Sea

Beijing

MING EMPIRE (CHINA)

Hwang Ho

Yangtze

Ningbo 1533–45
Fuzhou 1547–49
Canton (Guangzhou)
Macau 1555
St John Island 1550

ANNAM

Mekong

Salween

BURMA

SIAM

Ayutthaya

Syriam 1520–1613

Philippine Islands

South China Sea

Spice Islands (Moluccas)
Ternate 1512–74
Gilolo
Amboina (Ambon) 1511–99
Tidore 1522–74
Bacan Is 1558
Menado 1540
Celebes
Fort Larantuka 1557
Flores
Timor 1520

Makasar 1545–1667

Borneo

Java Sea

Bantam
Java 1522–96

Sumatra Strait

Melaka 1511–1641
Bintan I 1526–1628
Singapore 1526
Barus 1519
Acêh
Pasei 1520–24
1509 Pidie
1520 Acêh

Strait of Malacca

Sumatra

MUGHAL EMPIRE (INDIA)

Brahmaputra

Ganges

Indus

Delhi
Agra
Hooghly 1537–1640

Bay of Bengal

Masulipatam 1570–1605

Cambay 1539
Surat 1540–1615
Daman 1558
Diu 1535
Bombay 1530
Chaul 1509

Malabar Coast
1510 Goa
1505 Anjediva
1565 Mangalore 1560–1637 Bhatkal
1505 Cannanore
1510–1616 Calicut
1503 Cochin
1512 Quilon

Coromandel Coast

Jaffna 1560
Ceylon 1518
Batticaloa 1519–1638
Galle 1518–1640
1518 Colombo

Maldive Islands

Indian Ocean

Arabian Sea

SAFAVID EMPIRE (PERSIA)

Caspian Sea

Aral Sea

Bandar Abbas 1507–1622
Ormuz 1515–1622
Muscat 1550–1650
Bahrain Island 1515–1622

The Gulf

Socotra 1506–11

Gulf of Aden

Aden

Red Sea

Massawa

Black Sea

Mogadishu
Barawa
Malindi 1520
Mombasa 1505/28
Pemba 1520
Zanzibar 1503
Kilwa 1505
Mozambique 1507

Equator

32. Europeans in Asia

1500–1750

✳ ✳ ✳

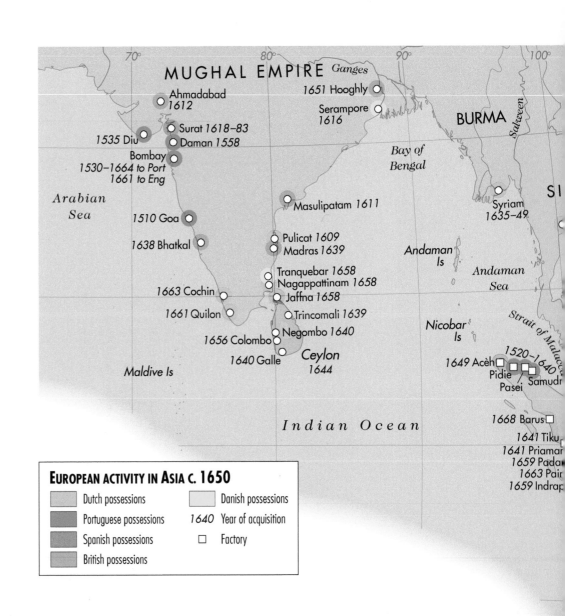

MUGHAL EMPIRE *Ganges*

1651 Hooghly

Serampore
1616

BURMA

*Bay of
Bengal*

Ahmadabad
1612

Surat 1618–83
1535 Diu
Daman 1558
Bombay
1530–1664 to Port
1661 to Eng

*Arabian
Sea*

1510 Goa

1638 Bhatkal

Masulipatam 1611

Syriam
1635–49

SI

Pulicat 1609
Madras 1639

*Andaman
Is*

*Andaman
Sea*

Tranquebar 1658
Nagappattinam 1658
1663 Cochin
Jaffna 1658
1661 Quilon
Trincomali 1639
Negombo 1640
1656 Colombo
*Nicobar
Is*

Strait of Malacca

1520–1640

1649 Acèh
Pidie
Pasei
Samudr

1640 Galle
Ceylon
1644

Maldive Is

Indian Ocean

1668 Barus
1641 Tiku
1641 Priaman
1659 Pada
1663 Pair
1659 Indrap

EUROPEAN ACTIVITY IN ASIA C. 1650

Dutch possessions	Danish possessions
Portuguese possessions	1640 Year of acquisition
Spanish possessions	☐ Factory
British possessions	

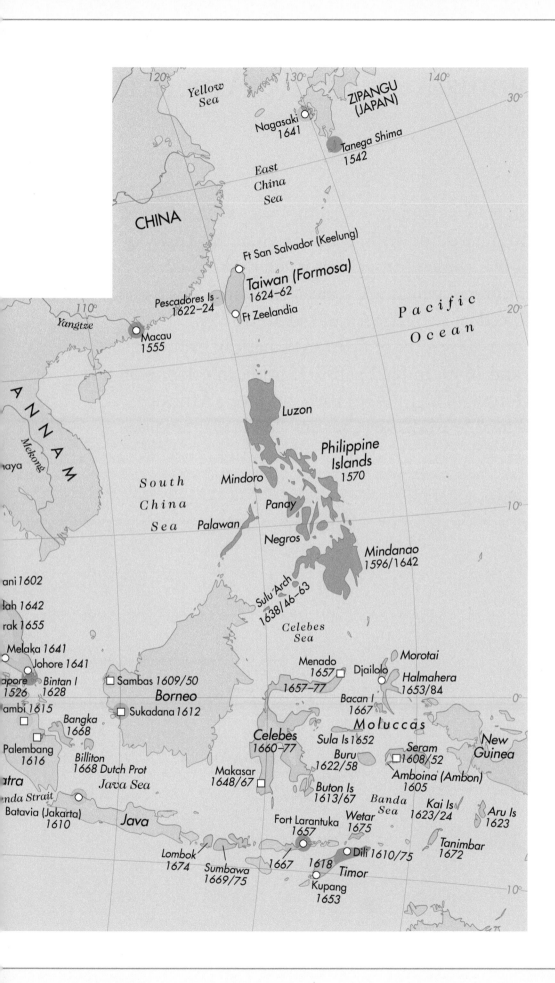

Yellow
Sea

ZIPANGU
(JAPAN)

30°

Nagasaki
1641

Tanega Shima
1542

East
China
Sea

CHINA

Ft San Salvador (Keelung)

Taiwan (Formosa)
1624–62

Pescadores Is
1622–24

Ft Zeelandia

Pacific
Ocean

20°

Yangtze

110°

Macau
1555

A N N A M

Mekong

naya

Luzon

Philippine
Islands
1570

South
China
Sea

Mindoro

Panay

10°

Palawan

Negros

Mindanao
1596/1642

ani 1602

Sulu Arch
1638/46–63

Celebes
Sea

Jah 1642

rak 1655

Melaka 1641

Menado
1657

Morotai

Djailolo

Johore 1641

☐ Sambas 1609/50

1657–77

Halmahera
1653/84

apore
1526

Bintan I
1628

Borneo

Bacan I
1667

0°

ambi 1615

☐

Bangka
1668

☐ Sukadana 1612

Moluccas

Palembang
1616

Billiton
1668 Dutch Prot
Java Sea

Celebes
1660–77

Sula Is 1652

Sula Is 1652

Seram
☐ 1608/52

New
Guinea

Buru
1622/58

atra

Makasar
1648/67 ☐

Buton Is
1613/67

Amboina (Ambon)
1605

Kai Is
1623/24

Aru Is
1623

nda Strait

Batavia (Jakarta)
1610

Java

Fort Larantuka
1657

Wetar
1675

Banda
Sea

Tanimbar
1672

Lombok
1674

Sumbawa
1669/75

1667

1618

Dili 1610/75

Timor

Kupang
1653

10°

33. The Colonization of the Americas

1500–1780

✳ ✳ ✳

The Spanish crown claimed sovereignty over all American territory to the west of the line laid down at the Treaty of Tordesillas in 1494, while Portugal was given the territory to the east. Silver mining, which was concentrated in Mexico and based on the forced labor of American Indian workers, accounted for over 90 percent of Spanish-American exports between 1550 and 1640. In the Spanish Caribbean colonies of Cuba, Santo Domingo, and Puerto Rico, however, African slave labor was used to work the sugar and coffee plantations.

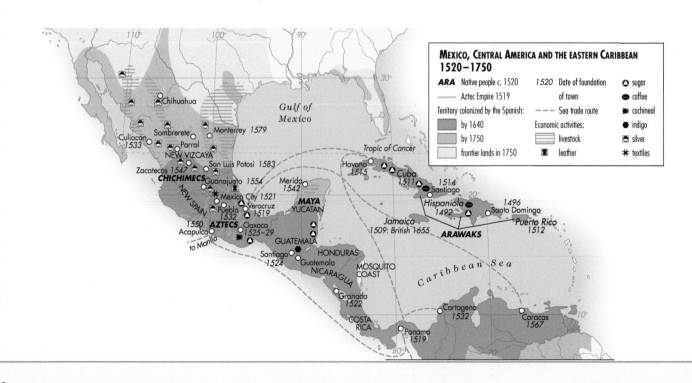

MEXICO, CENTRAL AMERICA AND THE EASTERN CARIBBEAN 1520–1750

ARA Native people c. 1520	*1520* Date of foundation of town	⬤ sugar
Aztec Empire 1519		⬤ coffee
Territory colonized by the Spanish:	– – – Sea trade route	✳ cochineal
by 1640	Economic activities:	⬤ indigo
by 1750	livestock	silver
frontier lands in 1750	leather	✳ textiles

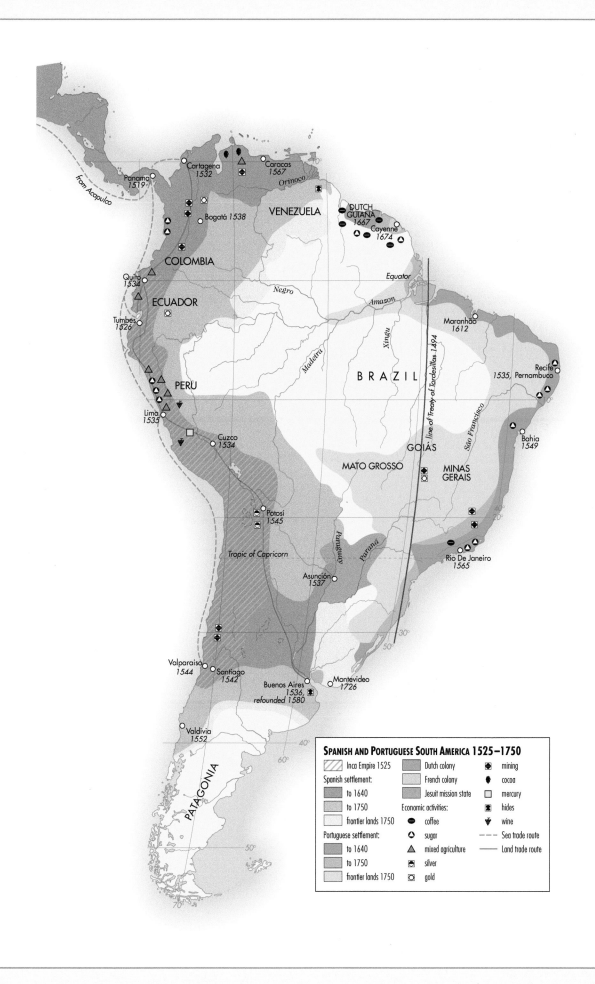

Panama
1519

from Acapulco

Cartagena
1532

Caracas
1567

Orinoco

VENEZUELA

DUTCH
GUIANA
1667

Cayenne
1674

Bogatá 1538

COLOMBIA

Quito
1534

ECUADOR

Negro

Equator

Amazon

Maranhão
1612

Tumbes
1526

Xingu

B R A Z I L

Recife
1535, Pernambuco

Madeira

line of Treaty of Tordesillas 1494

PERU

São Francisco

Bahia
1549

Lima
1535

Cuzco
1534

GOIÁS

MATO GROSSO

MINAS
GERAIS

Potosí
1545

Paraguay

Paraná

Rio De Janeiro
1565

Tropic of Capricorn

Asunción
1537

30°

50°

Valparaíso
1544

Santiago
1542

Buenos Aires
1536,
refounded 1580

Montevideo
1726

Valdivia
1552

40°

60°

PATAGONIA

50°

70°

SPANISH AND PORTUGUESE SOUTH AMERICA 1525–1750

▨ Inca Empire 1525	▨ Dutch colony	⬤ mining
Spanish settlement:	▨ French colony	⬢ cocoa
▨ to 1640	▨ Jesuit mission state	▢ mercury
▨ to 1750	**Economic activities:**	⬒ hides
▨ frontier lands 1750	⬤ coffee	⬘ wine
Portuguese settlement:	△ sugar	
▨ to 1640	△ mixed agriculture	– – – Sea trade route
▨ to 1750	⬓ silver	—— Land trade route
▨ frontier lands 1750	⬗ gold	

13

33. The Colonization of the Americas
1500–1780

✳ ✳ ✳

The Spanish Empire in North America was vast, but it attracted few settlers, and there was virtually no economic development outside Florida. The French Empire, although large, was thinly populated, and its limited economic development was based on fishing and the fur trade. By contrast, the British Empire had the least extensive territory, but it developed a rich, diverse, and populous economy and an extensive overseas trade.

COLONIZATION OF THE NORTH AMERICAN MAINLAND TO 1750

HUR Native American people

British settlement:
- to 1640
- to 1750
- frontier lands in 1750

Spanish settlement:
- to 1750
- frontier lands in 1750

French settlement:
- to 1750
- frontier lands in 1750

Economic activity c.1750:
- ◗ mixed agriculture
- ◖ fishing
- ▦ trapping
- ⬟ cattle
- ◉ grain
- ◉ tobacco
- ◑ rice
- ◆ indigo
- ▲ timber
- ⊥⊥⊥ shipbuilding
- ▢ ironworks
- → trade route

Santa Fe

El Paso

Rio Grande

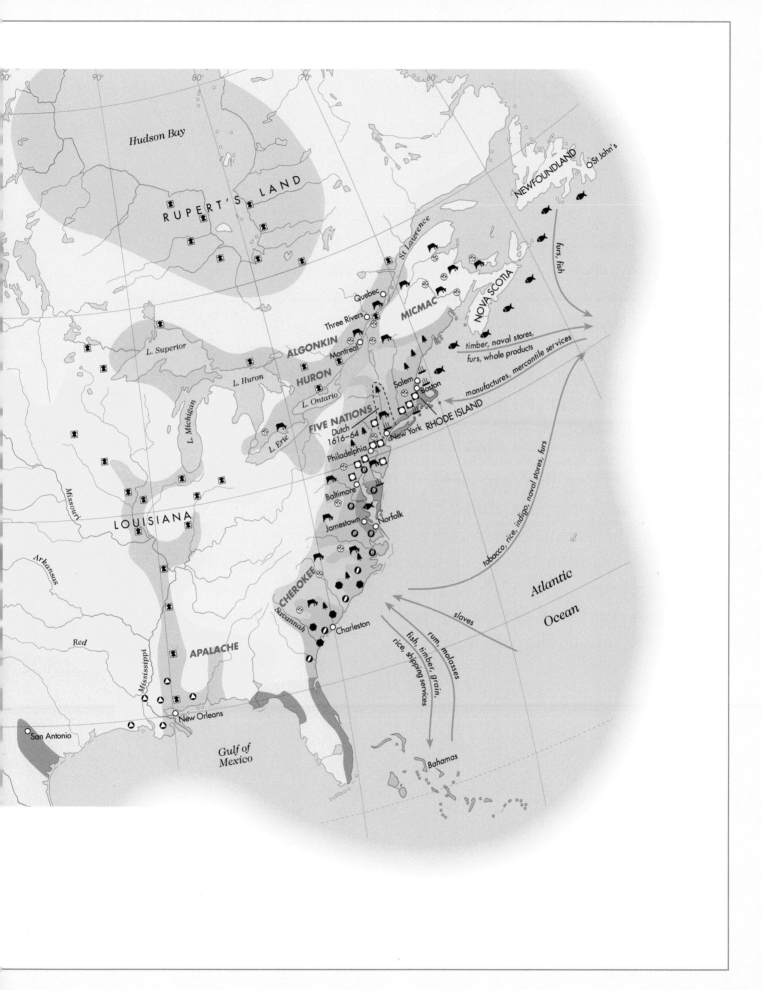

Hudson Bay

RUPERT'S LAND

NEWFOUNDLAND

O St John's

furs, fish

St Lawrence

Quebec

Three Rivers

MICMAC

NOVA SCOTIA

ALGONKIN

Montreal

HURON

timber, naval stores, furs, whale products

L. Superior

L. Huron

L. Ontario

L. Michigan

Salem

Boston

manufactures, mercantile services

L. Erie

FIVE NATIONS

Dutch 1616-64

New York

RHODE ISLAND

Philadelphia

Baltimore

Missouri

LOUISIANA

Jamestown

Norfolk

tobacco, rice, indigo, naval stores, furs

Arkansas

CHEROKEE

Atlantic

Ocean

Red

Savannah

APALACHE

Charleston

slaves

rum, molasses

fish, timber, grain, rice, shipping services

Mississippi

New Orleans

O San Antonio

Gulf of
Mexico

Bahamas

34. European States

1500–1600

* * *

Maps of 16th-century Europe are deceptive in that they appear to suggest that the western countries—France, Spain, and England—and the eastern countries—Poland and Russia—were consolidated and centralized, while sandwiched between them many tiny entities formed the Holy Roman Empire. In fact, all of the European states were highly decentralized and regionalized. France actually saw an increase in devolution during the 16th century as many provinces escaped control during the French Wars of Religion (1562–1598).

The ruling dynasties of Europe were all closely related to each other, though this did not prevent the fighting of wars. Many of these wars were pursued more for glory than for the annexation of territory or other gain. An example of these "wars of magnificence" is the conflict that plagued Italy during this period, with France and the Habsburgs both fighting over rival claims on the peninsula.

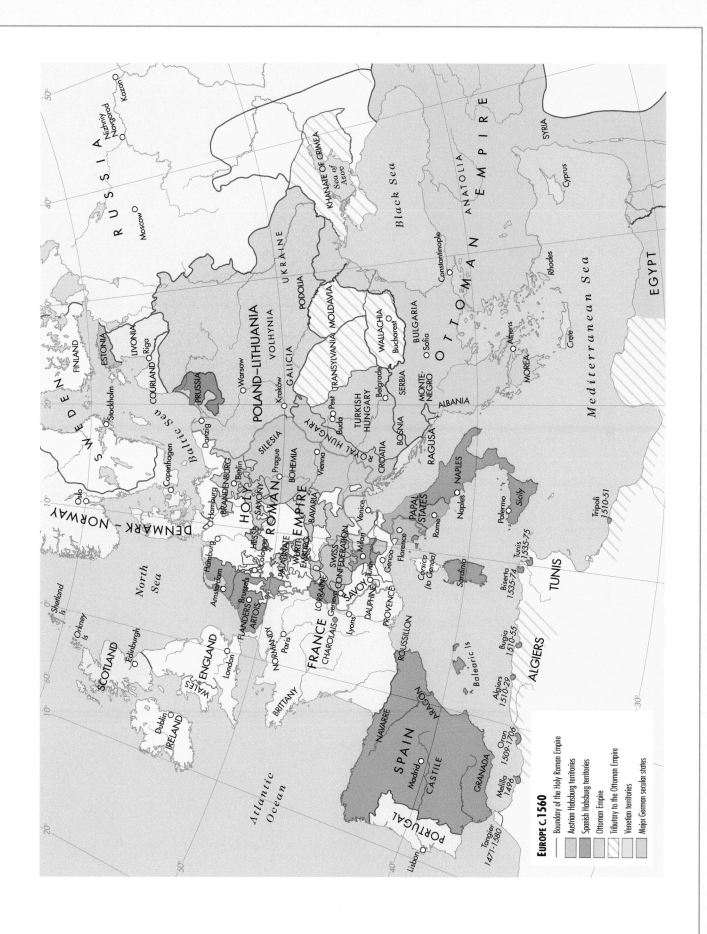

EUROPE c. 1560

— Boundary of the Holy Roman Empire
Austrian Habsburg territories
Spanish Habsburg territories
Ottoman Empire
Tributary to the Ottoman Empire
Venetian territories
Major German secular states

RUSSIA

Kazan

Nizhniy Novgorod

Moscow

FINLAND

SWEDEN

ESTONIA

LIVONIA   Riga

COURLAND

Stockholm

Copenhagen

DENMARK – NORWAY

Oslo

NORWAY

Shetland Is

Orkney Is

North Sea

SCOTLAND

Edinburgh

ENGLAND

WALES

London

IRELAND

Dublin

Atlantic Ocean

BRITTANY

NORMANDY

Paris

FRANCE

CHAROLAIS

Lyons

DAUPHINÉ

PROVENCE

Amsterdam

Brussels

FLANDERS

ARTOIS

Hamburg

Hamburg

Hesse

BRANDENBURG   Berlin

HOLY

ROMAN

SAXONY

BAVARIA

BOHEMIA   Prague

SILESIA

PALATINATE

WÜRTT-
EMBERG

SWISS
CONFEDERATION

Geneva

LORRAINE

SAVOY

Turin

Milan

Venice

Genoa

Florence

Corsica
(to Genoa)

Sardinia

PAPAL
STATES

Rome

Naples

NAPLES

Palermo

Sicily

Tunis
1535-74

Biserta
1535-55

TUNIS

Balearic Is

Bugia
1510-55

Algiers
1510-29

ALGIERS

SPAIN

Madrid

CASTILE

ARAGON

NAVARRE

GRANADA

Melilla
1498

Oran
1509-1706

PORTUGAL

Lisbon

Tangier
1471-1580

ROUSSILLON

Baltic Sea

PRUSSIA

Danzig

Warsaw

POLAND–LITHUANIA

Kraków

GALICIA

VOLHYNIA

PODOLIA

UKRAINE

KHANATE OF CRIMEA

Sea of
Azov

Black Sea

MOLDAVIA

TRANSYLVANIA

WALLACHIA

Bucharest

ROYAL HUNGARY

TURKISH
HUNGARY

Buda

Pest

Vienna

Belgrade

SERBIA

BOSNIA

CROATIA

RAGUSA

MONTE-
NEGRO

ALBANIA

BULGARIA

Sofia

OTTOMAN EMPIRE

ANATOLIA

Constantinople

SYRIA

Cyprus

Rhodes

Athens

MOREA

Crete

Mediterranean Sea

EGYPT

Tripoli
1510-51

17

34. European States

1500–1600

✳ ✳ ✳

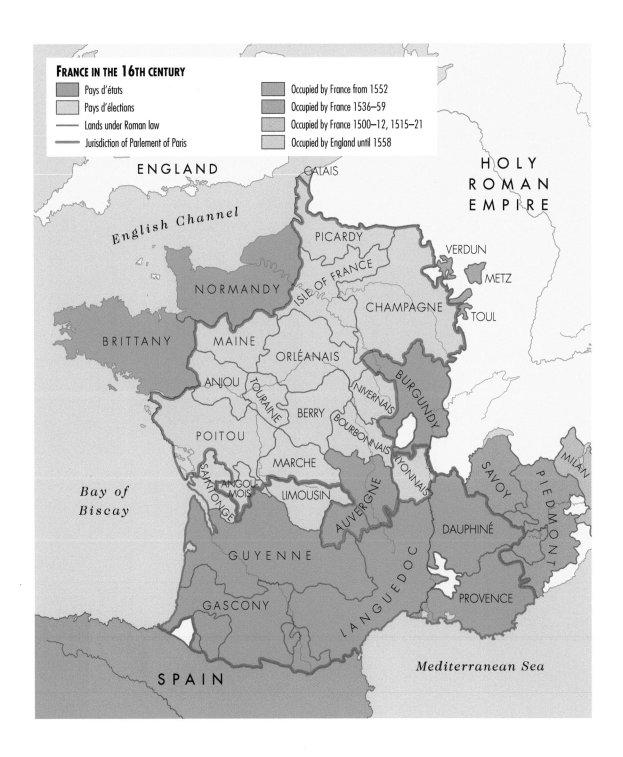

FRANCE IN THE 16TH CENTURY

- Pays d'états
- Pays d'élections
- Lands under Roman law
- Jurisdiction of Parlement of Paris
- Occupied by France from 1552
- Occupied by France 1536–59
- Occupied by France 1500–12, 1515–21
- Occupied by England until 1558

ENGLAND

CALAIS

English Channel

PICARDY

VERDUN

METZ

ISLE OF FRANCE

NORMANDY

CHAMPAGNE

TOUL

HOLY ROMAN EMPIRE

BRITTANY

MAINE

ORLÉANAIS

NIVERNAIS

BURGUNDY

ANJOU

TOURAINE

BERRY

BOURBONNAIS

POITOU

MARCHE

LYONNAIS

SAINTONGE

ANGOU-MOIS

LIMOUSIN

AUVERGNE

SAVOY

PIEDMONT

MILAN

Bay of
Biscay

DAUPHINÉ

GUYENNE

LANGUEDOC

GASCONY

PROVENCE

SPAIN

Mediterranean Sea

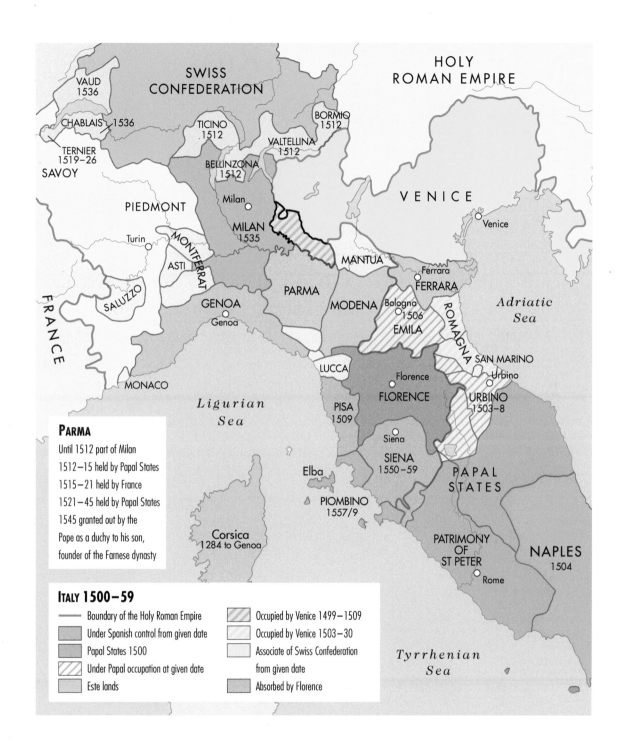

VAUD
1536

SWISS
CONFEDERATION

HOLY
ROMAN EMPIRE

CHABLAIS 1536

TICINO
1512

BORMIO
1512

TERNIER
1519–26

VALTELLINA
1512

SAVOY

BELLINZONA
1512

PIEDMONT

Milan

VENICE

Venice

Turin

MILAN
1535

MONTFERRAT

ASTI

MANTUA

Ferrara

FRANCE

SALUZZO

PARMA

MODENA

FERRARA

*Adriatic
Sea*

GENOA

Bologna
1506

ROMAGNA

Genoa

EMILA

SAN MARINO

LUCCA

Florence

Urbino

MONACO

*Ligurian
Sea*

PISA
1509

FLORENCE

URBINO
1503–8

PARMA

Until 1512 part of Milan

1512–15 held by Papal States

1515–21 held by France

1521–45 held by Papal States

1545 granted out by the

Pope as a duchy to his son,

founder of the Farnese dynasty

Elba

Siena

SIENA
1550–59

PAPAL
STATES

PIOMBINO
1557/9

Corsica
1284 to Genoa

PATRIMONY
OF
ST PETER

NAPLES
1504

Rome

ITALY 1500–59

— Boundary of the Holy Roman Empire

   Under Spanish control from given date

   Papal States 1500

   Under Papal occupation at given date

   Este lands

   Occupied by Venice 1499–1509

   Occupied by Venice 1503–30

   Associate of Swiss Confederation
   from given date

   Absorbed by Florence

*Tyrrhenian
Sea*

35. The Expansion of Russia and Sweden

1462–1795

✳ ✳ ✳

Russian expansion eastward involved the establishment of *ostrogs* (fortified trading posts) at strategic points. An *ostrog* was founded at Tomsk in 1604, and by 1607 Turuchansk on the Yenisei River had been reached. The river became the frontier of the empire in 1619, with another string of *ostrogs* being established along it.

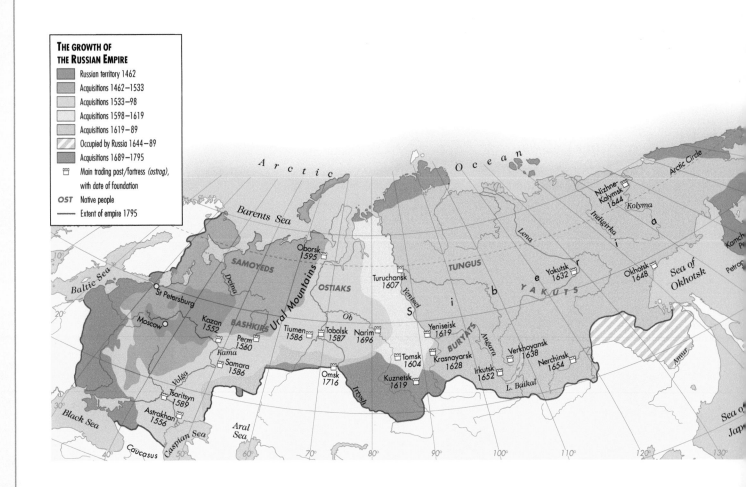

THE GROWTH OF THE RUSSIAN EMPIRE

- Russian territory 1462
- Acquisitions 1462–1533
- Acquisitions 1533–98
- Acquisitions 1598–1619
- Acquisitions 1619–89
- Occupied by Russia 1644–89
- Acquisitions 1689–1795
- ⌂ Main trading post/fortress (ostrog), with date of foundation
- OST Native people
- —— Extent of empire 1795

Arctic Ocean

Arctic Circle

Barents Sea

Oborsk 1595

SAMOYEDS

Pechora

Ural Mountains

OSTIAKS

Turuchansk 1607

TUNGUS

Lena

Nizhne-Kolymsk 1644

Kolyma

Indigirka

Baltic Sea

St Petersburg

Yakutsk 1632

YAKUTS

Okhotsk 1648

Sea of Okhotsk

Kamch. Pen.

Petro...

Moscow

Kazan 1552

BASHKIRS

Ob

Tiumen 1586

Tobolsk 1587

Narim 1696

Yeniseisk 1619

Yenisei

Angara

Verkhoyansk 1638

Perm 1560

Kama

Samara 1586

Omsk 1716

Tomsk 1604

Krasnoyarsk 1628

BURYATS

Irkutsk 1652

L. Baikal

Nerchinsk 1654

Amur

Volga

Tsaritsyn 1589

Irtosh

Kuznetsk 1619

Astrakhan 1556

Black Sea

Caucasus

Aral Sea

Caspian Sea

Sea of Japan

SWEDISH EXPANSION IN THE 16TH AND 17TH CENTURIES

- Sweden 1560
- Swedish acquisitions 1560–1660
- Swedish colonization in Finland
- Swedish occupation of Russia 1613
- Denmark–Norway
- Occupied first by Denmark, then Sweden 1645
- Seas and lakes frozen in winter
- ● Personal royal union with date
- — Principal trade route
- ○ Hanseatic port 1500
- Iron mining
- Copper mining
- Silver mining
- Gold mining

In the 16th century Sweden was a small country of just over a million people. However, with the aid of its natural resources, it built a Baltic empire, reaching the summit of its power between 1621 and 1660.

36. The Reformation and Counter-Reformation

✳ ✳ ✳

Protestantism took a number of forms across Europe. In Germany and Scandinavia local secular rulers promoted the establishment of new churches, mostly along Lutheran lines. In the Netherlands, Calvinism became politically predominant during the later 16th century, while in England the Anglican Church was established by Henry VIII. Further east, Calvinism was adopted in Transylvania (in Hungary), and in Poland so many nobles became Protestant that special provisions for their toleration had to be agreed in 1569–1571. Switzerland was a major powerhouse of the Protestant Reformation but was intensely divided. French Protestantism was overwhelmingly urban. Crucial to its survival, however, was the support of a very large minority of the nobility.

THE PROTESTANT AND CATHOLIC REFORMATIONS

- Reformed faith dominant by 1580
- Reformed faith growing c. 1560–70
- Considerable local reformed faith c. 1560–70
- Some penetration of reform c. 1560–70
- Remained predominantly Catholic

- Lutheranism formally established, with date
- Calvinism or Zwinglianism formally established, with date
- Protestantism formally tolerated by 1580
- Anglican (predominantly Calvinist) Church established, with date

- Anabaptists, Mennonites and Melchiorites
- † Catholic mission and reform endeavour, with date
- 187 Number of legates sent to the last session of the Council of Trent (by country or region)

36. The Reformation and Counter-Reformation

✳ ✳ ✳

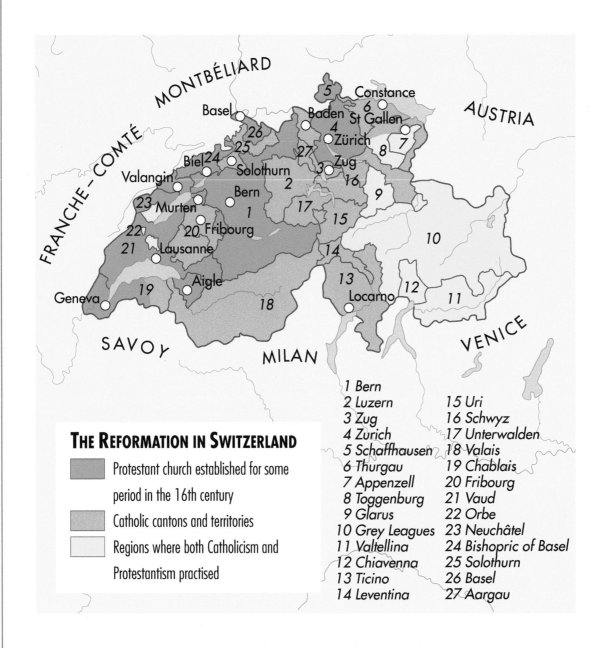

THE REFORMATION IN SWITZERLAND

Protestant church established for some period in the 16th century

Catholic cantons and territories

Regions where both Catholicism and Protestantism practised

1 Bern
2 Luzern
3 Zug
4 Zürich
5 Schaffhausen
6 Thurgau
7 Appenzell
8 Toggenburg
9 Glarus
10 Grey Leagues
11 Valtellina
12 Chiavenna
13 Ticino
14 Leventina

15 Uri
16 Schwyz
17 Unterwalden
18 Valais
19 Chablais
20 Fribourg
21 Vaud
22 Orbe
23 Neuchâtel
24 Bishopric of Basel
25 Solothurn
26 Basel
27 Aargau

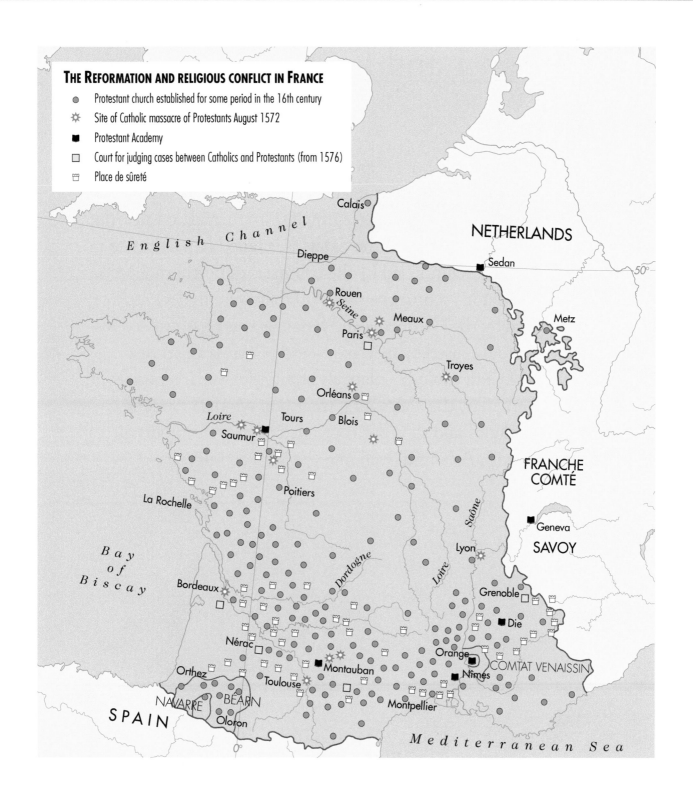

THE REFORMATION AND RELIGIOUS CONFLICT IN FRANCE

- Protestant church established for some period in the 16th century
- Site of Catholic massacre of Protestants August 1572
- Protestant Academy
- Court for judging cases between Catholics and Protestants (from 1576)
- Place de sûreté

Calais

English Channel

NETHERLANDS

Dieppe

Sedan

50°

Rouen

Seine

Meaux

Metz

Paris

Troyes

Orléans

Loire

Tours

Blois

Saumur

FRANCHE COMTÉ

Poitiers

La Rochelle

Saône

Geneva

Lyon

SAVOY

Bay of Biscay

Dordogne

Loire

Grenoble

Bordeaux

Die

Nérac

Orange

COMTAT VENAISSIN

Orthez

Montauban

Nîmes

Toulouse

Montpellier

NAVARRE

BÉARN

SPAIN

Oloron

Mediterranean Sea

37. Eurasian Land Empires

ca. 1700

✳ ✳ ✳

Despite periods of vigorous territorial and economic expansion, the great land empires of western and southern Eurasia—the Ottomans, the Mughals, and the Safavids—failed to participate in the commercial revolution led by the countries of northern Europe in the 17th and 18th centuries—by 1700 they were in decline. The territory ruled by the Ottomans and Safavids was criss-crossed by land and sea routes used by merchants and pilgrims alike. Sea travel was risky but could be relatively straightforward, especially in regions governed by the alternating monsoon winds. Overland traffic was arduous and slow but continued to play an important role in trade with Asia until well into the 18th century.

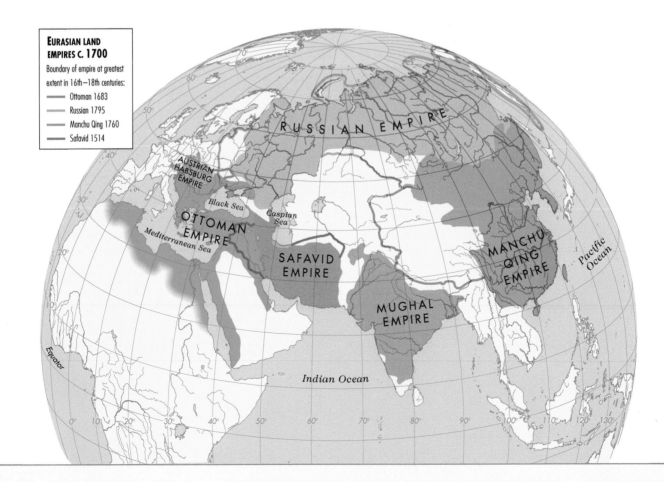

EURASIAN LAND EMPIRES C. 1700

Boundary of empire at greatest extent in 16th–18th centuries:

——— Ottoman 1683
——— Russian 1795
——— Manchu Qing 1760
——— Safavid 1514

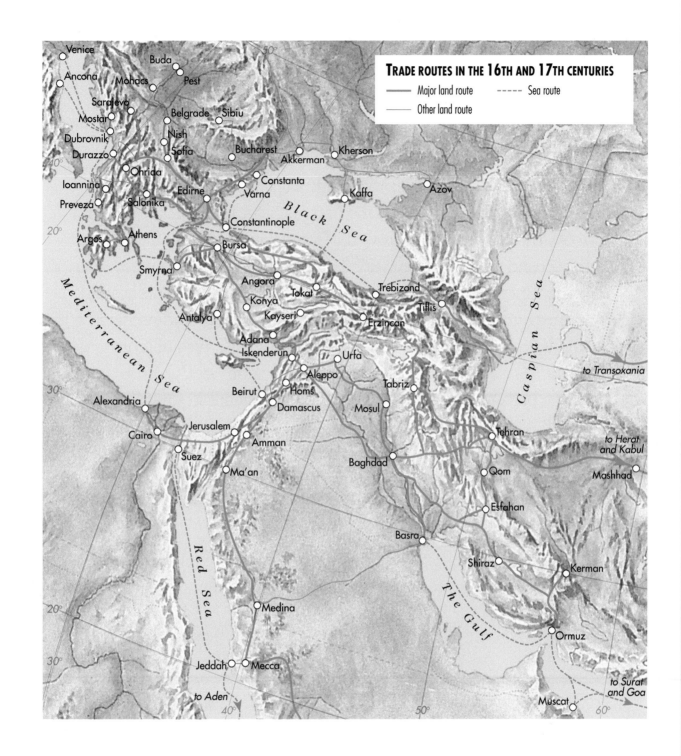

TRADE ROUTES IN THE 16TH AND 17TH CENTURIES

——— Major land route ------ Sea route
——— Other land route

Venice
Ancona
Buda
Mohacs
Pest
Sarajevo
Mostar
Belgrade
Sibiu
Dubrovnik
Nish
Durazzo
Sofia
Bucharest
Akkerman
Kherson
Ohrida
Ioannina
Edirne
Constanta
Kaffa
Azov
Preveza
Salonika
Varna
Argos
Athens
Constantinople
Black Sea
Bursa
Smyrna
Angora
Tokat
Trebizond
Konya
Kayseri
Tiflis
Antalya
Erzincan
Adana
Iskenderun
Urfa
Tabriz
Aleppo
Beirut
Homs
Mosul
Damascus
Alexandria
Jerusalem
Amman
Baghdad
Tehran
to Herat and Kabul
Cairo
Qom
Mashhad
Suez
Ma'an
Esfahan
Basra
Shiraz
Kerman
Red Sea
Caspian Sea
to Transoxania
The Gulf
Medina
Ormuz
Jeddah
Mecca
to Surat and Goa
to Aden
Muscat
Mediterranean Sea

20°
30°
40°
50°
60°

27

38. European Urbanization

1500–1700

✳ ✳ ✳

The process of urbanization in Europe involved three overlapping phases. In the first of these, from 1500 to around 1650, there was general growth of towns and cities of all sizes. In the second phase, between 1650 and 1750, a few large cities—most notably London, Paris, and Amsterdam—expanded rapidly, while in the third phase there was an increase in the size and number of smaller cities and a relative leveling off in the growth of larger cities. In the 16th century the most urbanized regions in Europe—defined by the percentage of the total population resident in towns and cities—were the northern and southern Netherlands and Italy. From the early 17th century, however, urban growth subsided in the last two regions while cities in the northern Netherlands expanded rapidly, as did those of England and Scotland. By comparison, only moderate urbanization took place in France.

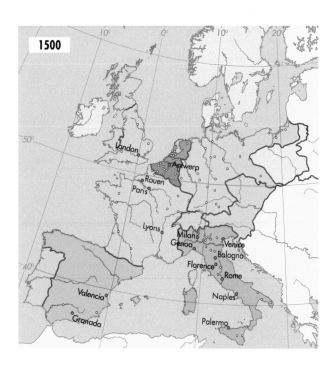

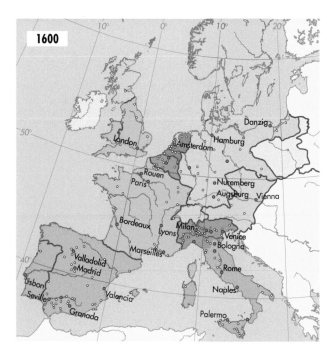

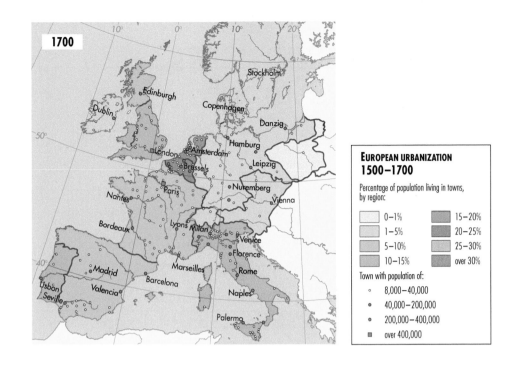

1700

Stockholm
Edinburgh
Dublin
Copenhagen
Danzig
Hamburg
London
Amsterdam
Brussels
Leipzig
Nantes
Paris
Nuremberg
Vienna
Bordeaux
Lyons
Milan
Venice
Madrid
Marseilles
Florence
Barcelona
Rome
Lisbon
Valencia
Naples
Seville
Palermo

EUROPEAN URBANIZATION 1500–1700

Percentage of population living in towns, by region:

- 0–1%
- 1–5%
- 5–10%
- 10–15%
- 15–20%
- 20–25%
- 25–30%
- over 30%

Town with population of:

- ○ 8,000–40,000
- ◦ 40,000–200,000
- ● 200,000–400,000
- ■ over 400,000

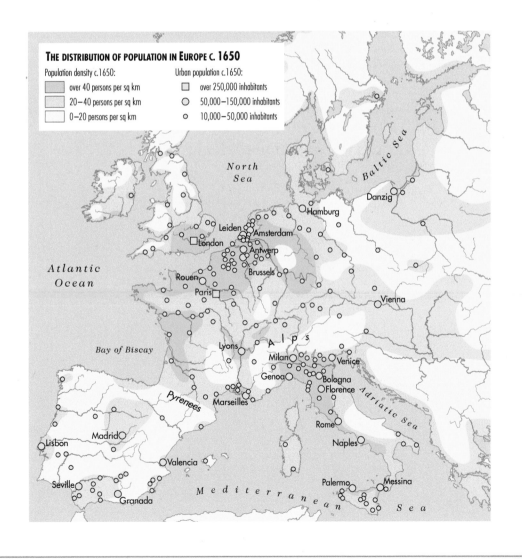

THE DISTRIBUTION OF POPULATION IN EUROPE C. 1650

Population density c.1650:

- over 40 persons per sq km
- 20–40 persons per sq km
- 0–20 persons per sq km

Urban population c.1650:

- □ over 250,000 inhabitants
- ○ 50,000–150,000 inhabitants
- ○ 10,000–50,000 inhabitants

North Sea
Baltic Sea
Danzig
Hamburg
Leiden
Amsterdam
London
Antwerp
Brussels
Atlantic Ocean
Rouen
Paris
Vienna
Bay of Biscay
Lyons
A l p s
Milan
Venice
Genoa
Bologna
Florence
Adriatic Sea
Pyrenees
Marseilles
Rome
Madrid
Naples
Lisbon
Valencia
Palermo
Messina
Seville
Granada
M e d i t e r r a n e a n   S e a

39. The Development of Science and Technology in Europe

✳ ✳ ✳

From the mid-16th century botanical gardens were established in many university towns, and in the following century academies of science added a new dimension to the range of institutions that promoted learning. From the 1650s the air pump was developed in a number of European cities. The first Newcomen engine was installed in 1712 at Dudley Castle in Staffordshire, and the design was quickly taken up by coalfields and other mining operations across the north of England.

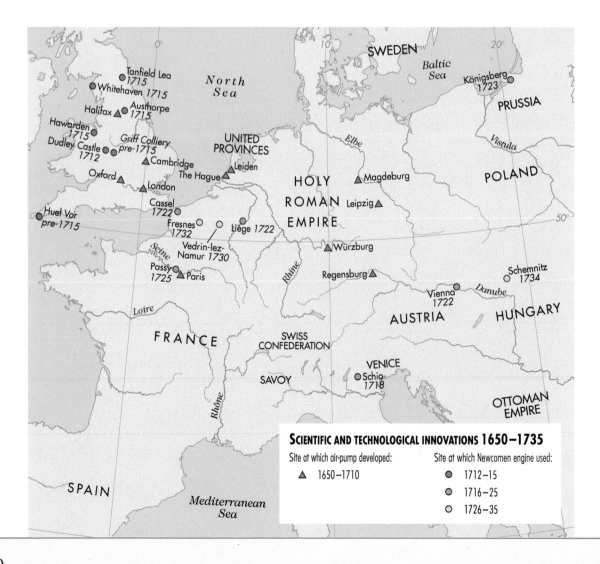

SCIENTIFIC AND TECHNOLOGICAL INNOVATIONS 1650–1735

Site at which air-pump developed:
▲ 1650–1710

Site at which Newcomen engine used:
● 1712–15
● 1716–25
○ 1726–35

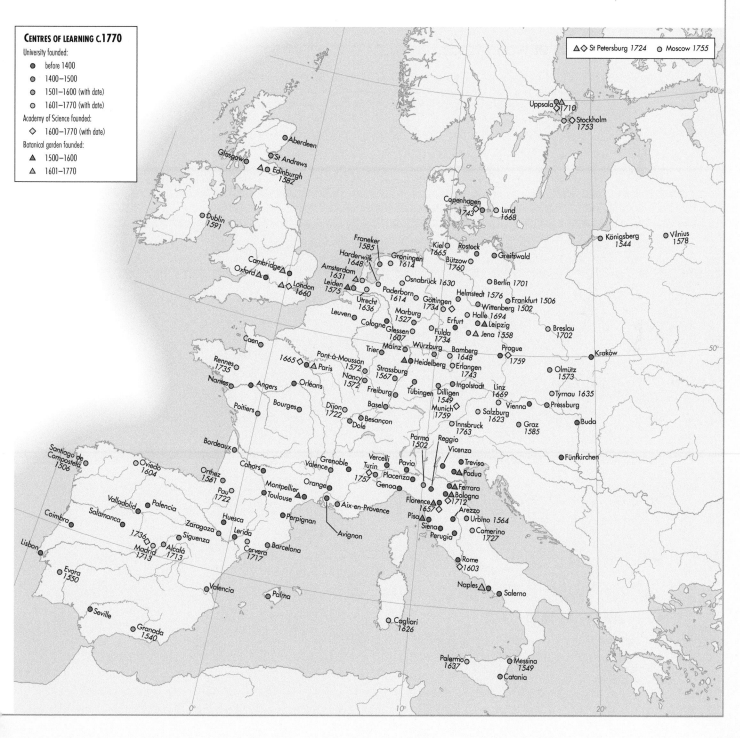

CENTRES OF LEARNING c.1770

University founded:
- ● before 1400
- ● 1400–1500
- ● 1501–1600 (with date)
- ○ 1601–1770 (with date)

Academy of Science founded:
- ◇ 1600–1770 (with date)

Botanical garden founded:
- ▲ 1500–1600
- △ 1601–1770

△◇ St Petersburg *1724*   ◎ Moscow *1755*

Uppsala *1710*
Stockholm *1753*

Copenhagen *1743*   Lund *1668*

Aberdeen
Glasgow   St Andrews
Edinburgh *1582*

Vilnius *1578*
Königsberg *1544*

Dublin *1591*

Franeker *1585*
Kiel *1665*   Rostock   Greifswald
Harderwijk *1648*   Groningen *1614*   Bützow *1760*
Cambridge   Amsterdam *1631*   Osnabrück *1630*   Berlin *1701*
Oxford   Leiden *1575*   Paderborn *1614*   Helmstedt *1576*   Frankfurt *1506*
London *1660*   Utrecht *1636*   Göttingen *1734*   Wittenberg *1502*   Breslau *1702*
Leuven   Marburg *1527*   Halle *1694*
Cologne   Glessen *1607*   Erfurt   Leipzig   Jena *1558*
Caen   Fulda *1734*
Trier   Mainz   Würzburg   Bamberg   Prague *1759*   Kraków
Rennes *1735*   Pont-à-Mousson *1572*   Heidelberg   Erlangen *1743*   Olmütz *1573*
Paris   Strassburg *1567*   Nancy *1572*
Nantes   Angers   Orléans   Freiburg   Tübingen   Dilligen *1549*   Linz *1669*   Tyrnau *1635*
Poitiers   Bourges   Dijon *1722*   Basel   Munich *1759*   Ingolstadt   Vienna   Pressburg
Besançon   Salzburg *1623*   Graz *1585*   Buda
Dole   Innsbruck *1763*
Bordeaux   Parma *1502*   Reggio   Vicenza   Fünfkirchen
Santiago de Compostela *1506*   Oviedo *1604*   Grenoble   Vercelli   Pavia   Treviso
Cahors   Valence   Turin   Placenza   Padua
Orthez *1561*   Orange   Genoa   Ferrara
Pau *1722*   Montpellier   *1757*   Bologna *1712*
Valladolid   Palencia   Toulouse   Florence *1657*
Coimbra   Huesca   Aix-en-Provence   Pisa   Arezzo   Urbino *1564*
Salamanca   Zaragoza   Perpignan   Siena   Camerino *1727*
Lisbon   Lerida   Barcelona   Perugia
Madrid *1713*   Siguenza   Avignon
1736   Alcalá *1713*   Cervera *1717*
Evora *1550*   Rome   *1603*
Valencia   Palma   Naples   Salerno
Seville
Granada *1540*   Cagliari *1626*

Palermo *1637*   Messina *1549*
Catania

31

40. European Empires and Trade

✳ ✳ ✳

In the 17th and 18th centuries the countries of northwest Europe were at the center of an expanding world economy. Fueled in large part by slave labor imported from Africa, silver from the mines of Central and South America reached Europe via Spain and Portugal, where it entered the arteries of world trade.

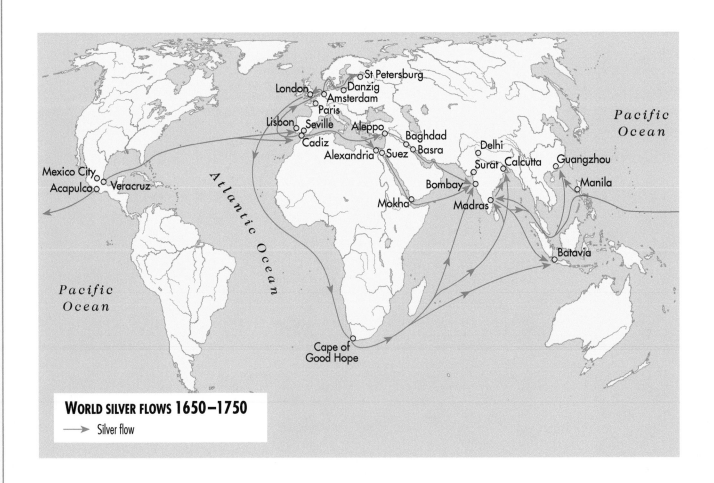

WORLD SILVER FLOWS 1650–1750

→ Silver flow

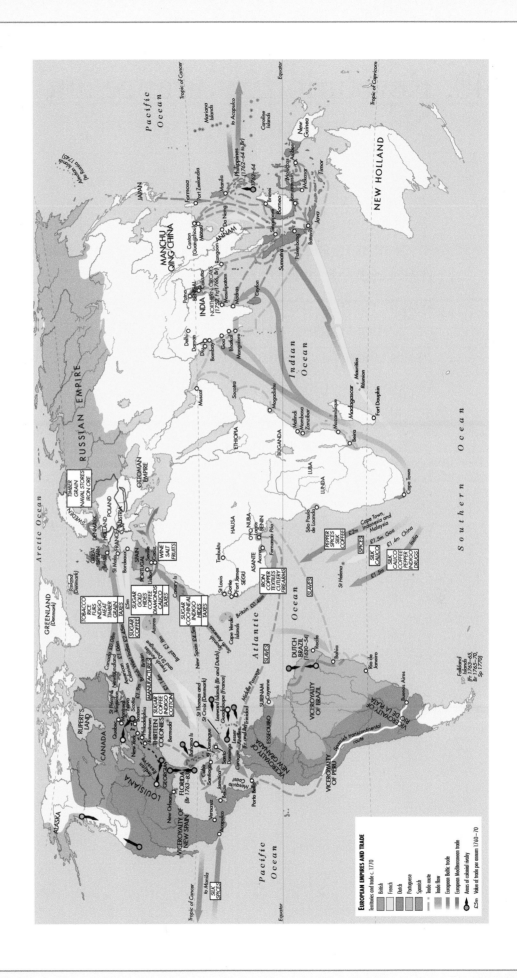

EUROPEAN EMPIRES AND TRADE

Territories and trade c. 1770

- British
- French
- Dutch
- Portuguese
- Spanish
- Trade route
- Trade flow
- European Baltic trade
- European Mediterranean trade
- Areas of colonial rivalry
- Value of trade per annum 1760–70
- £5m

RUSSIAN EMPIRE

OTTOMAN EMPIRE

MANCHU QING CHINA

JAPAN

INDIA

NEW HOLLAND

GREENLAND (Denmark)

CANADA

RUPERT'S LAND

ALASKA

LOUISIANA

THIRTEEN COLONIES

FLORIDA (Br 1763–83)

GEORGIA

VICEROYALTY OF NEW SPAIN

VICEROYALTY OF NEW GRANADA

VICEROYALTY OF PERU

VICEROYALTY OF BRAZIL

VICEROYALTY OF RÍO DE LA PLATA

ESSEQUIBO
SURINAM

DUTCH BRAZIL (1630–54)

ETHIOPIA

BUGANDA

LUBA

LUNDA

HAUSA

OYO NUBA
BENIN
ASANTE

Cape Town Indonesia and Malaysia

Pacific Ocean

Atlantic Ocean

Indian Ocean

Arctic Ocean

Southern Ocean

Tropic of Cancer
Tropic of Capricorn
Equator

TIMBER
GRAIN
NAVAL STORES
IRON ORE

TOBACCO
RICE
FURS
INDIGO
MEAT
TIMBER
GRAIN
TAXES

SUGAR
GOLD
HIDES
COFFEE
DIAMONDS
CALICO
TAXES

SUGAR
COCHINEAL
HIDES
TAXES

WINE
SALT
FRUITS

SUGAR
COFFEE

MANUFACTURES

SUGAR
COFFEE
INDIGO
COTTON

IRON
COPPER
TEXTILES
CUTLERY
FIREARMS

SLAVES

SLAVES

PEPPER
SPICES
SILK
COFFEE £2m

SPICES

SILK
CALICO

SILK
CALICO
COFFEE
PEPPER
INDIGO
DRUGS

£1 .4m China
£1.5m Goa
£1.5m India

SILK
SPICES

to Manila

to Acapulco

33

41. Revolutionary France and Napoleonic Europe

✳ ✳ ✳

Napoleon's armies waged war across Europe in an attempt to impose French rule and the Civil Code throughout the continent. The turning point in his fortune came in 1812 when, with an army already fighting in Spain, he embarked on a disastrous invasion of Russia. From 1793 onward the rulers of the European states formed various alliances in an attempt to counter the threat from France.

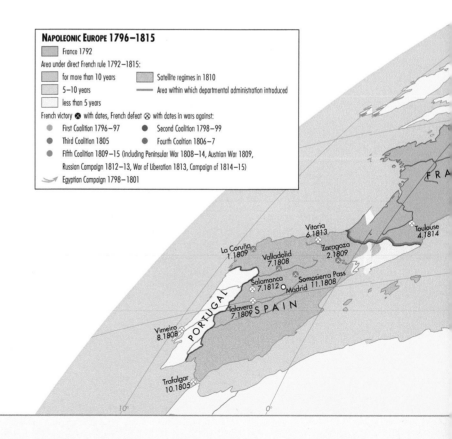

NAPOLEONIC EUROPE 1796–1815

☐ France 1792

Area under direct French rule 1792–1815:

☐ for more than 10 years   ☐ Satellite regimes in 1810

☐ 5–10 years   —— Area within which departmental administration introduced

☐ less than 5 years

French victory ✸ with dates, French defeat ⊗ with dates in wars against:

● First Coalition 1796–97   ● Second Coalition 1798–99

● Third Coalition 1805   ● Fourth Coalition 1806–7

● Fifth Coalition 1809–15 (including Peninsular War 1808–14, Austrian War 1809, Russian Campaign 1812–13, War of Liberation 1813, Campaign of 1814–15)

⤳ Egyptian Campaign 1798–1801

Vitoria 6.1813

Toulouse 4.1814

La Coruña 1.1809

Valladolid 7.1808

Zaragoza 2.1809

Salamanca 7.1812   Somosierra Pass

Madrid 11.1808

Talavera 7.1809 SPAIN

PORTUGAL

Vimeiro 8.1808

Trafalgar 10.1805

FRA

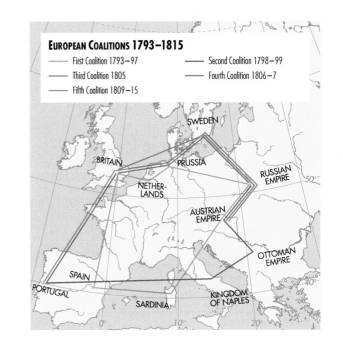

SWEDEN

BRITAIN   PRUSSIA   RUSSIAN EMPIRE

NETHER-LANDS

AUSTRIAN EMPIRE

OTTOMAN EMPIRE

SPAIN

PORTUGAL

SARDINIA   KINGDOM OF NAPLES

North Sea

Baltic Sea

Copenhagen

Königsberg

PRUSSIA

Friedland 6.1807

Warsaw

Vitebsk 7.1812

Borodino 9.1812

Moscow 9–10.1812

Borisov 11.1812

Krasnoj 11.1812

Maloyaroslavets 10.1812

RUSSIAN EMPIRE

Leipzig 10.1813

Berlin 10.1806

NETHERLANDS

Jena 10.1806

Dresden 8.1813

GRAND DUCHY OF WARSAW

Brussels

Waterloo 6.1815

CONFEDERATION OF THE RHINE

Austerlitz 12.1805

Montmirail 2.1814

Ulm 10.1805

Regensburg 4.1809

Hollabrun 11.1805

Aspern and Essling 5.1809

Wagram 7.1809

Vienna

Buda   Pest

Zürich 6.1799

Hohenlinden 12.1800

AUSTRIAN EMPIRE

Lodi 5.1796

Rivoli 11.1796

Marengo 6.1800

Mantua 6.1796

KINGDOM OF ITALY

Belgrade

Mondovi 4.1796

Novi 8.1799

Ancona 2.1797

OTTOMAN EMPIRE

TUSCANY

Adriatic Sea

Elba

Rome

KINGDOM OF NAPLES

Naples

RDINIA

ured and held gion 1798–1801

Mediterranean Sea

42. The Industrial Revolution

✳ ✳ ✳

In 1750 most English people lived in the countryside. The largest center of manufacturing was London, whose population had increased from an estimated 120,000 to 675,000 between 1550 and 1750. Britain, with its head start, steamed ahead of the rest of Europe in terms of industrial output per capita in the first half of the 19th century, but Belgium, with readily available sources of coal and iron ore, also experienced an increase in output of more than 100 percent. Germany started comparatively slowly but increased the volume of its industrial production per person by 240 percent between 1880 and 1913.

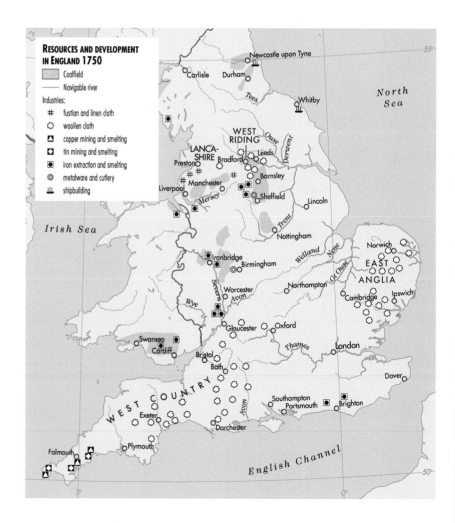

RESOURCES AND DEVELOPMENT IN ENGLAND 1750

- Coalfield
- Navigable river

Industries:
- # fustian and linen cloth
- ✿ woollen cloth
- ▲ copper mining and smelting
- ◹ tin mining and smelting
- ◉ iron extraction and smelting
- ✤ metalware and cutlery
- �Ⅲ shipbuilding

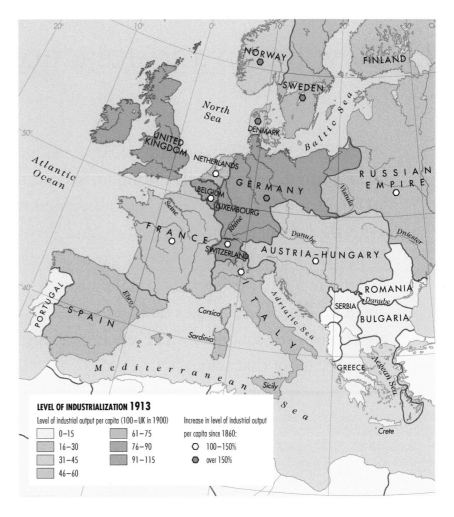

LEVEL OF INDUSTRIALIZATION **1913**

Level of industrial output per capita (100 = UK in 1900)

☐ 0–15	☐ 61–75
☐ 16–30	☐ 76–90
☐ 31–45	☐ 91–115
☐ 46–60	

Increase in level of industrial output per capita since 1860:

- ◯ 100–150%
- ⬡ over 150%

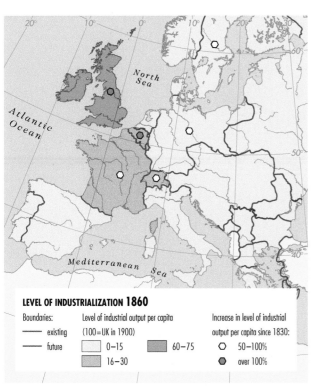

LEVEL OF INDUSTRIALIZATION **1860**

Boundaries:
— existing
— future

Level of industrial output per capita (100 = UK in 1900)

☐ 0–15	☐ 60–75
☐ 16–30	

Increase in level of industrial output per capita since 1830:

- ◯ 50–100%
- ⬡ over 100%

43. Revolution and Reaction in Europe

✳ ✳ ✳

During the 1820s and early 1830s rebellions broke out across Europe, with liberals calling for an end to absolute monarchy in Spain and Portugal and in the Italian peninsula. The Greeks, with the help of the French, British, and Russians, drove out the Ottomans. The Russians also intervened to crush rebellion in Poland in 1830, having defeated their own Decembrist Revolution in 1825. Rebellions broke out again across Europe in 1848, inspired by the success of the French in abolishing their monarchy in February of that year.

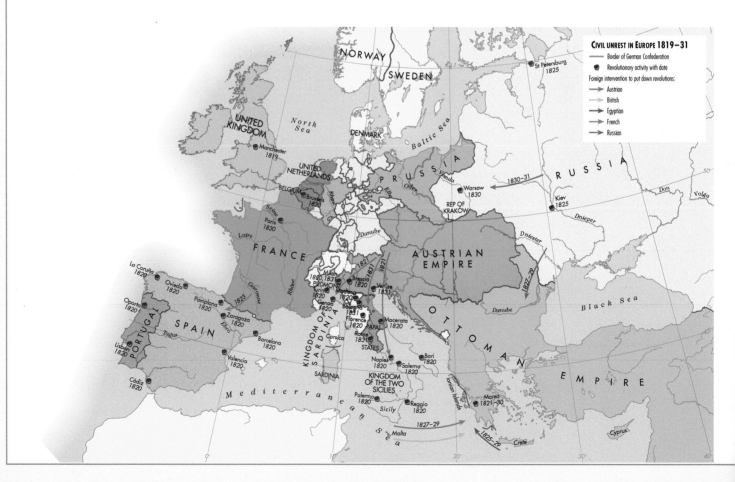

CIVIL UNREST IN EUROPE 1819–31

— Border of German Confederation
● Revolutionary activity with date

Foreign intervention to put down revolutions:
→ Austrian
→ British
→ Egyptian
→ French
→ Russian

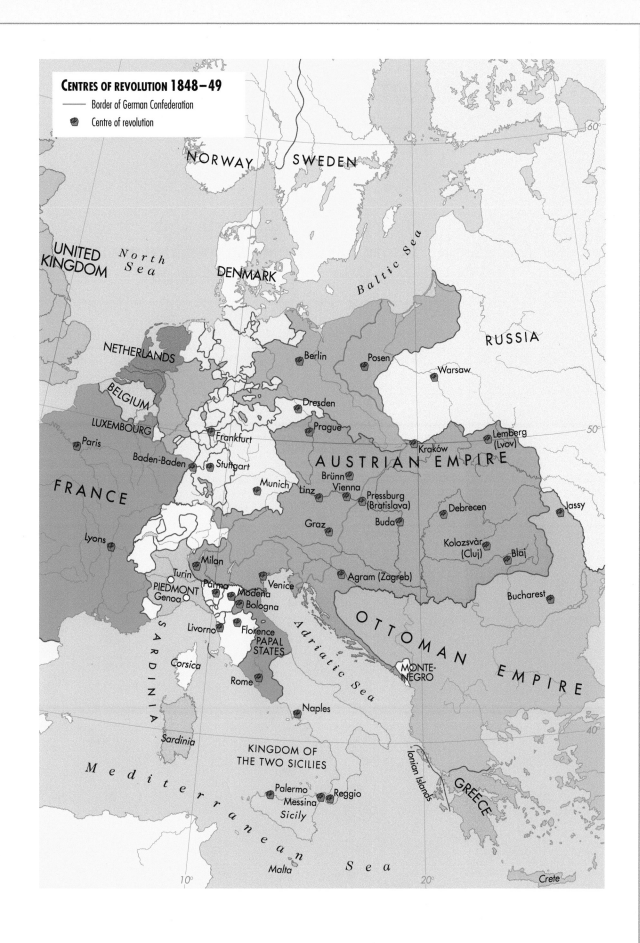

CENTRES OF REVOLUTION 1848–49

— Border of German Confederation

🖐 Centre of revolution

NORWAY

SWEDEN

UNITED KINGDOM

North Sea

DENMARK

Baltic Sea

RUSSIA

NETHERLANDS

BELGIUM

LUXEMBOURG

Berlin

Posen

Warsaw

Dresden

Frankfurt

Prague

Lemberg (Lvov)

Kraków

Paris

Baden-Baden

Stuttgart

AUSTRIAN EMPIRE

FRANCE

Munich

Linz

Brünn

Vienna

Pressburg (Bratislava)

Debrecen

Jassy

Graz

Buda

Lyons

Kolozsvàr (Cluj)

Blaj

Milan

Turin

PIEDMONT

Genoa

Parma

Modena

Bologna

Venice

Agram (Zagreb)

Bucharest

Livorno

Florence

PAPAL STATES

Adriatic Sea

OTTOMAN EMPIRE

SARDINIA

Corsica

Rome

MONTE-NEGRO

Sardinia

Naples

Ionian Islands

KINGDOM OF THE TWO SICILIES

GREECE

Mediterranean Sea

Palermo

Messina

Reggio

Sicily

Malta

Crete

39

44. The Ottoman and Habsburg Empires—Expansion and Decline

✳ ✳ ✳

The Ottoman Empire reached its furthest extent in the mid-17th century, but when its troops failed to take Vienna in 1683, European powers took advantage of their disarray and seized territory in central Europe. The subsequent disintegration of the empire took place over the next 240 years.

In 1815 the Austrian Habsburgs regained territory lost during the Napoleonic Wars. However, they were forced to give it up in the mid-19th century during the process of Italian unification, and in 1867 they were persuaded to grant Hungary equal status to that of Austria.

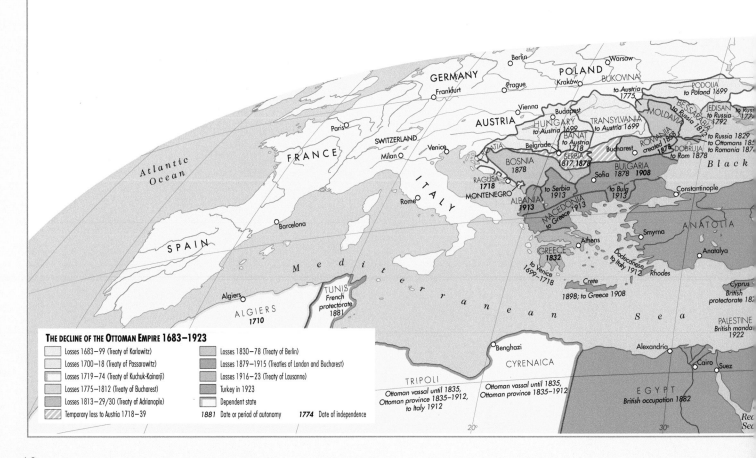

THE DECLINE OF THE OTTOMAN EMPIRE 1683–1923

- Losses 1683–99 (Treaty of Karlowitz)
- Losses 1700–18 (Treaty of Passarowitz)
- Losses 1719–74 (Treaty of Kuchuk-Kainarji)
- Losses 1775–1812 (Treaty of Bucharest)
- Losses 1813–29/30 (Treaty of Adrianople)
- Temporary loss to Austria 1718–39
- Losses 1830–78 (Treaty of Berlin)
- Losses 1879–1915 (Treaties of London and Bucharest)
- Losses 1916–23 (Treaty of Lausanne)
- Turkey in 1923
- Dependent state
- *1881* Date or period of autonomy
- **1774** Date of independence

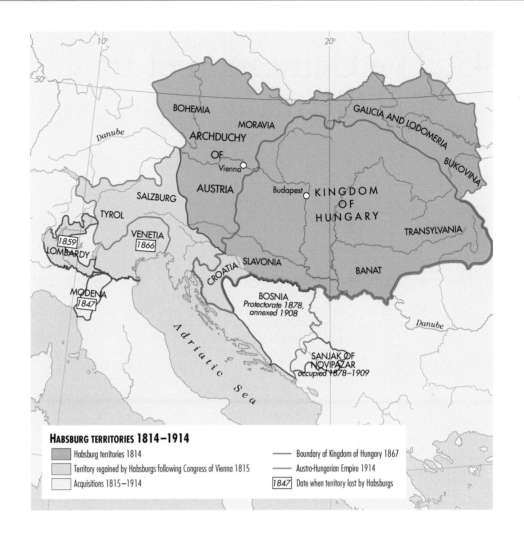

HABSBURG TERRITORIES 1814–1914

Danube

50°

BOHEMIA

MORAVIA

ARCHDUCHY

OF

○ Vienna

GALICIA AND LODOMERIA

BUKOVINA

AUSTRIA

Budapest ○

KINGDOM
OF
HUNGARY

SALZBURG

TYROL

VENETIA
1866

TRANSYLVANIA

1859

LOMBARDY

CROATIA

SLAVONIA

BANAT

MODENA
1847

BOSNIA
*Protectorate 1878,
annexed 1908*

A d r i a t i c   S e a

Danube

SANJAK OF
NOVIPAZAR
occupied 1878–1909

■ Habsburg territories 1814	— Boundary of Kingdom of Hungary 1867
■ Territory regained by Habsburgs following Congress of Vienna 1815	— Austro-Hungarian Empire 1914
□ Acquisitions 1815–1914	*1847* Date when territory lost by Habsburgs

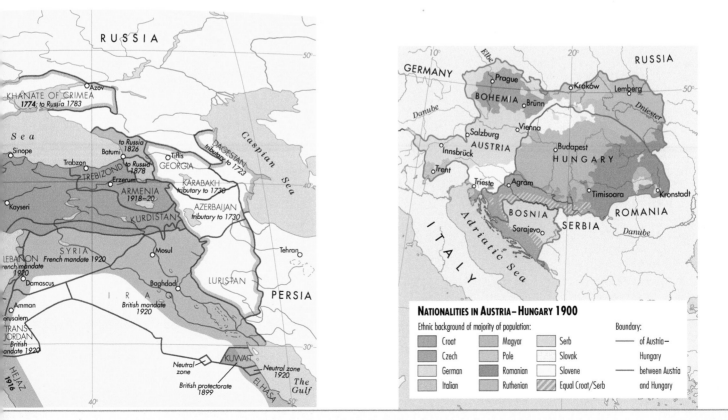

RUSSIA

KHANATE OF CRIMEA
1774; to Russia 1783

○ Azov

Sea

○ Sinope

Trabzon

Batumi
*to Russia
1826*

TREBIZOND
*to Russia
1878*

Erzerum

○ Tiflis

GEORGIA

DAGESTAN
tributary to 1723

Caspian Sea

50°

40°

KARABAKH
tributary to 1730

ARMENIA
1918–20

KURDISTAN

AZERBAIJAN
tributary to 1730

○ Kayseri

SYRIA

○ Mosul

○ Tehran

LURISTAN

LEBANON *French mandate 1920*
*French mandate
1920*

○ Damascus

I R A Q

PERSIA

○ Amman

○ Jerusalem

TRANS-
JORDAN
*British
mandate 1920*

○ Baghdad

*British mandate
1920*

HEJAZ
1916

*Neutral
zone*

KUWAIT

*Neutral zone
1920*

EL HASA

*British protectorate
1899*

The
Gulf

40°

30°

NATIONALITIES IN AUSTRIA–HUNGARY 1900

GERMANY

Elbe

RUSSIA

50°

○ Prague

BOHEMIA

○ Kraków

Lemberg ○

Danube

○ Brünn

Dniester

Salzburg ○

○ Vienna

Innsbrück ○

AUSTRIA

Budapest ○

HUNGARY

Trent ○

Trieste ○

Agram ○

○ Timisoara

Kronstadt ○

A d r i a t i c   S e a

BOSNIA

ROMANIA

I T A L Y

Sarajevo ○

SERBIA

Danube

Ethnic background of majority of population:

■ Croat	■ Magyar	■ Serb	Boundary:
■ Czech	■ Pole	▨ Slovak	— of Austria–
□ German	■ Romanian	□ Slovene	Hungary
■ Italian	■ Ruthenian	▨ Equal Croat/Serb	— between Austria
			and Hungary

41

45. The Unification of Italy and Germany

✳ ✳ ✳

SWITZERLAND

AUSTRIAN EMPIRE

SAVOY

Drava

LOMBARDY

VENETIA

Sava

Magenta 1859 · Milan
PIEDMONT
Solferino 1859

Villafranca · Venice

Turin 1861

Po

OTTOMAN EMPIRE

Parma
PARMA
MODENA
Modena

Genoa

Ravenna

FRANCE

A d r i a t i c   S e a

NICE
Nice
MONACO

MASSA
LUCCA

Florence 1865

SAN MARINO

MONACO

Livorno

TUSCANY

Castelfidardo 1860

PAPAL STATES

K I N G D O M   O F   S A R D I N I A

Corsica

Talamone

Tiber

PATRIMONY OF ST PETER

Rome 1870

Volturno 1860

KINGDOM OF THE TWO SICILIES

SARDINIA

Naples

Cagliari

Messina

Palermo

Milazzo 1860

Reggio

Calatafimi 1860

SICILY

THE UNIFICATION OF ITALY 1859–70

▦	Kingdom of Sardinia
▦	Ceded by Austria 1859
▨	Ceded to France 1860
▢	United with Piedmont 1860
▢	Ceded by Austria 1866
▢	Occupied by Italy 1870
1861	Date at which cities became capital of Italy
→	Expeditions of Piedmontese 1860
→	Route of Garibaldi's Thousand 1860
✗	Battle with date

Among the most important developments in 19th-century Europe was the unification of Italy and Germany as nation-states—a process that fundamentally altered the balance of power in the continent.

THE GERMAN CONFEDERATION, AUSTRIAN EMPIRE, PRUSSIA AND DENMARK 1815

▨ Austrian Habsburg Empire	—	Border of German Confederation
▨ Prussia		Denmark

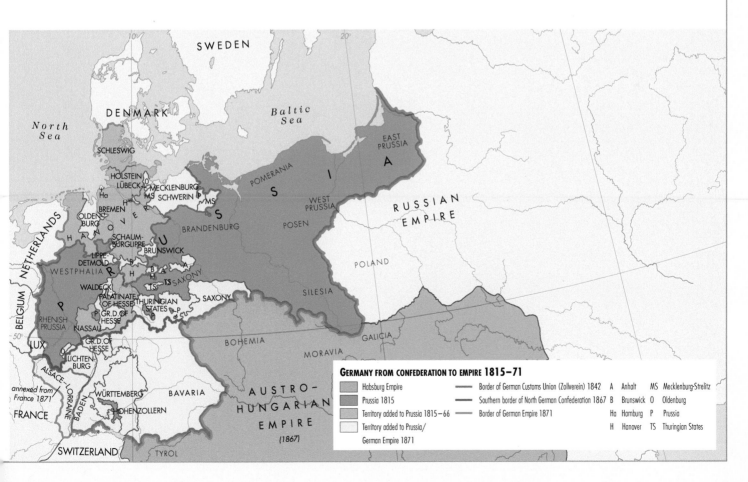

GERMANY FROM CONFEDERATION TO EMPIRE 1815–71

▨ Habsburg Empire	— Border of German Customs Union (Zollverein) 1842	A	Anhalt	MS	Mecklenburg-Strelitz
▨ Prussia 1815	— Southern border of North German Confederation 1867	B	Brunswick	O	Oldenburg
▨ Territory added to Prussia 1815–66	— Border of German Empire 1871	Ha	Hamburg	P	Prussia
▨ Territory added to Prussia/ German Empire 1871		H	Hanover	TS	Thuringian States

46. Russian Territorial and Economic Expansion

✳ ✳ ✳

Between 1795 and 1914 Russia sought to expand its territory in all possible directions but met with resistance from Austria, Britain, and France when it threatened their interests in the Balkans in the 1850s. To the east, the Russian Empire extended even to the continent of North America as far as northern California, until Alaska was sold to the Americans in 1867. To the southeast, Russia continued to exert its influence in Manchuria and Mongolia in the early years of the 20th century despite its defeat at the hands of the Japanese in 1905. ✦

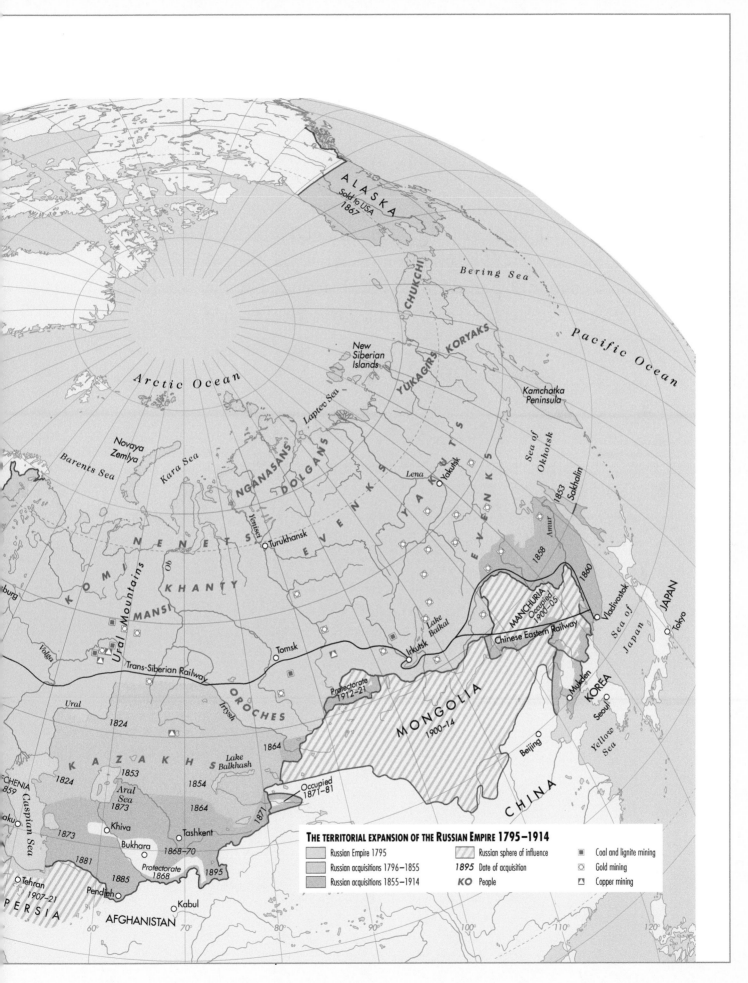

ALASKA
Sold to USA
1867

Bering Sea

Pacific Ocean

CHUKCHI

New
Siberian
Islands

YUKAGIRS KORYAKS

Kamchatka
Peninsula

Arctic Ocean

Laptev Sea

Novaya
Zemlya

Barents Sea

Kara Sea

NGANASANS

DOLGANS

EVENKS

YAKUTS

Lena   Yakutsk

EVENKS

Sea of
Okhotsk

1853 Sakhalin

Yenisei

Turukhansk

Ob

Amur

1858

KOMI NENETS

Ural Mountains

KHANTY

MANSI

Irtysh

Lake
Baikal

Irkutsk

1860

MANCHURIA
Occupied
1900–05

Vladivostok

JAPAN

burg

Volga

Trans-Siberian Railway

OROCHES

Tomsk

Chinese Eastern Railway

Sea of
Japan

Tokyo

Ural

1824

Protectorate
1912–21

MONGOLIA
1900–14

Mukden

KOREA

Seoul

CHENIA
1859

KAZAKHS

1824

1853

Lake
Balkhash

1864

Occupied
1871–81

Beijing

Yellow
Sea

CHINA

Aral
Sea
1873

Caspian Sea

1854

1864

1871

aku

1873

Khiva

Bukhara

Tashkent

1868–70

THE TERRITORIAL EXPANSION OF THE RUSSIAN EMPIRE 1795–1914

1881

Protectorate
1868

1895

Russian Empire 1795

Russian sphere of influence

Coal and lignite mining

Tehran

1907–21

Pendjeh

1885

Russian acquisitions 1796–1855

1895 Date of acquisition

Gold mining

PERSIA

AFGHANISTAN

Kabul

Russian acquisitions 1855–1914

KO People

Copper mining

60°   70°   80°   90°   100°   110°   120°

47. Africa

1840–1914

✳ ✳ ✳

In the mid-19th century European traders operated from bases on the African coast, supplied with goods by the African trading network. The partition of Africa was formalized at the Congress of Berlin (1884–1885), attended by the major European powers. The "Scramble for Africa" ensued.

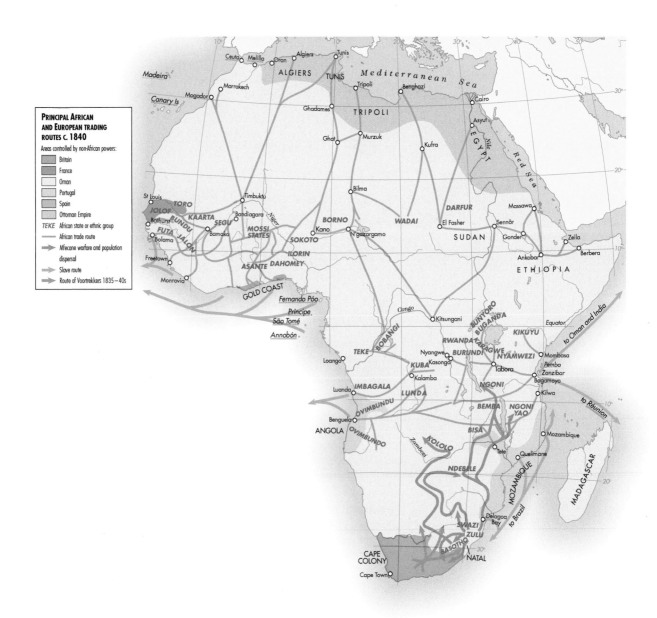

PRINCIPAL AFRICAN AND EUROPEAN TRADING ROUTES C. 1840

Areas controlled by non-African powers:
- Britain
- France
- Oman
- Portugal
- Spain
- Ottoman Empire

TEKE African state or ethnic group

— African trade route

→ Mfecane warfare and population dispersal

→ Slave route

→ Route of Voortrekkers 1835–40s

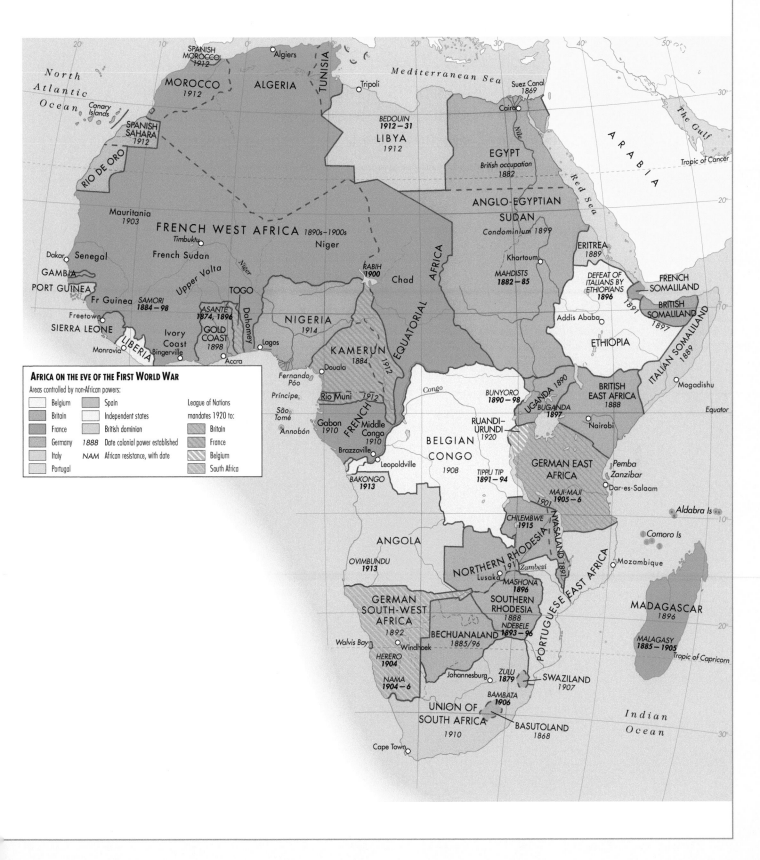

North Atlantic Ocean

Mediterranean Sea

ARABIA

The Gulf

SPANISH MOROCCO *1912*
Algiers
TUNISIA
Tripoli
MOROCCO *1912*
ALGERIA
BEDOUIN **1912–31**
LIBYA *1912*
Suez Canal *1869*
Cairo
EGYPT
British occupation *1882*
Tropic of Cancer

SPANISH SAHARA *1912*
RIO DE ORO
Canary Islands
Mauritania *1903*
FRENCH WEST AFRICA *1890s–1900s*
Niger
ANGLO-EGYPTIAN SUDAN
Condominium *1899*
Red Sea

Dakar
Senegal
Timbuktu
French Sudan
Upper Volta
Niger
RABIH **1900**
Chad
Khartoum
MAHDISTS **1882–85**
ERITREA *1889*
DEFEAT OF ITALIANS BY ETHIOPIANS **1896**
FRENCH SOMALILAND

GAMBIA
PORT GUINEA
Fr Guinea
SAMORI **1884–98**
TOGO
ASANTE **1874, 1896**
Dahomey
NIGERIA *1914*
KAMERUN *1884*
EQUATORIAL AFRICA
Addis Ababa
BRITISH SOMALILAND *1897*
ITALIAN SOMALILAND *1889*

Freetown
SIERRA LEONE
LIBERIA
Monrovia
Ivory Coast
Bingerville
GOLD COAST *1898*
Accra
Lagos
Douala
Fernando Póo
ETHIOPIA
Mogadishu

Príncipe
São Tomé
Rio Muni *1912*
FRENCH *1912*
Gabon *1910*
Middle Congo *1910*
Brazzaville
Congo
BUNYORO **1890–98**
UGANDA *1890*
BUGANDA *1897*
RUANDI-URUNDI *1920*
BRITISH EAST AFRICA *1888*
Nairobi
Equator

Annobón
BAKONGO **1913**
Leopoldville
BELGIAN CONGO *1908*
TIPPU TIP **1891–94**
GERMAN EAST AFRICA
Pemba
Zanzibar
Dar-es-Salaam
Aldabra Is

ANGOLA
OVIMBUNDU **1913**
MAJI-MAJI **1905–6**
CHILEMBWE **1915**
NYASALAND *1891*
PORTUGUESE EAST AFRICA
Comoro Is
Mozambique

GERMAN SOUTH-WEST AFRICA *1892*
Walvis Bay
Windhoek
HERERO **1904**
NAMA **1904–6**
NORTHERN RHODESIA *1911*
Lusaka
Zambesi
MASHONA **1896**
SOUTHERN RHODESIA *1888*
NDEBELE **1893–96**
BECHUANALAND *1885/96*
Johannesburg
ZULU **1879**
SWAZILAND *1907*
MADAGASCAR *1896*
MALAGASY **1885–1905**
Tropic of Capricorn

BAMBATA **1906**
UNION OF SOUTH AFRICA *1910*
BASUTOLAND *1868*
Indian Ocean
Cape Town

Africa on the eve of the First World War

Areas controlled by non-African powers:

Belgium	Spain
Britain	Independent states
France	British dominion
Germany	*1888* Date colonial power established
Italy	**NAM** African resistance, with date
Portugal	

League of Nations mandates 1920 to:
Britain
France
Belgium
South Africa

48. The British in India

✳ ✳ ✳

The expansion of British power in India was piecemeal. As frontiers of Britain's empire in India slowly stabilized, more than a third of the subcontinent remained governed by Indian rulers, although the British used trade and defense agreements to exert their influence over these areas.

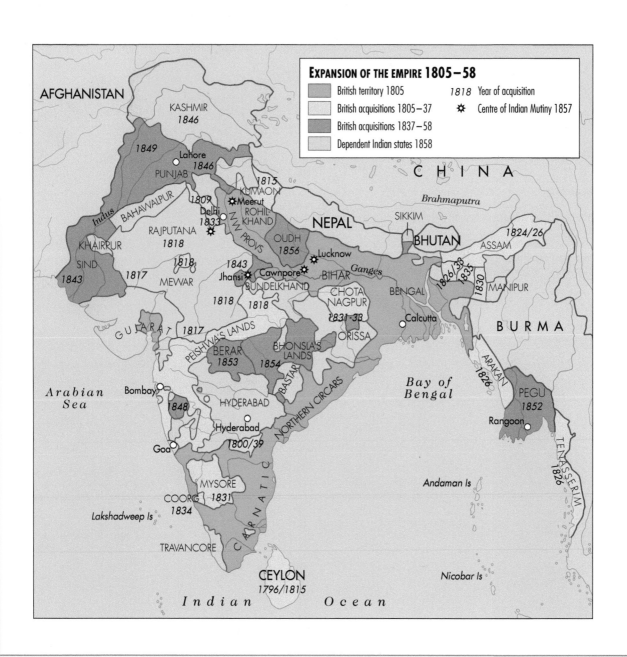

EXPANSION OF THE EMPIRE 1805–58

- British territory 1805
- British acquisitions 1805–37
- British acquisitions 1837–58
- Dependent Indian states 1858

1818 Year of acquisition
✿ Centre of Indian Mutiny 1857

AFGHANISTAN

KASHMIR
1846

1849

Lahore
1846

PUNJAB

CHINA

1815
KUMAON

1809
Delhi
1833

BAHAWALPUR

Indus

ROHIL-KHAND

✿Meerut

Brahmaputra

SIKKIM

1824/26

RAJPUTANA
1818

N.W. PROVS

OUDH
1856

NEPAL

BHUTAN

ASSAM

KHAIRPUR

1818

✿Lucknow

1826/38

1835

1830

MANIPUR

SIND
1843

1817

MEWAR

1843
Jhansi ✿

Cawnpore ✿

BIHAR

Ganges

BENGAL

1818   *1818*

BUNDELKHAND

CHOTA
NAGPUR

BURMA

GUJARAT *1817*

PEISHWA'S LANDS

1831–33

Calcutta

ORISSA

Arabian
Sea

Bombay

BERAR
1853

BHONSLA'S
LANDS
1854

BASTAR

NORTHERN CIRCARS

Bay of
Bengal

ARAKAN
1826

PEGU
1852

1848

HYDERABAD

Rangoon

Hyderabad

1800/39

Goa

Andaman Is

TENASSERIM
1826

MYSORE

COORG
1834

1831

CARNATIC

Lakshadweep Is

TRAVANCORE

CEYLON
1796/1815

Nicobar Is

Indian   Ocean

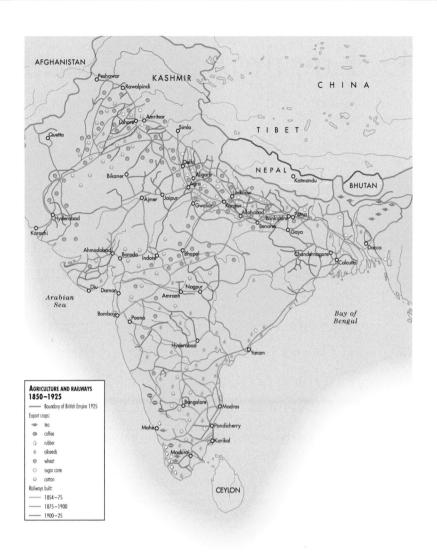

AGRICULTURE AND RAILWAYS 1850–1925

— Boundary of British Empire 1925

Export crops:
- 🍵 tea
- ☕ coffee
- ○ rubber
- ◔ oilseeds
- ◉ wheat
- ○ sugar cane
- ○ cotton

Railways built:
— 1854–75
— 1875–1900
— 1900–25

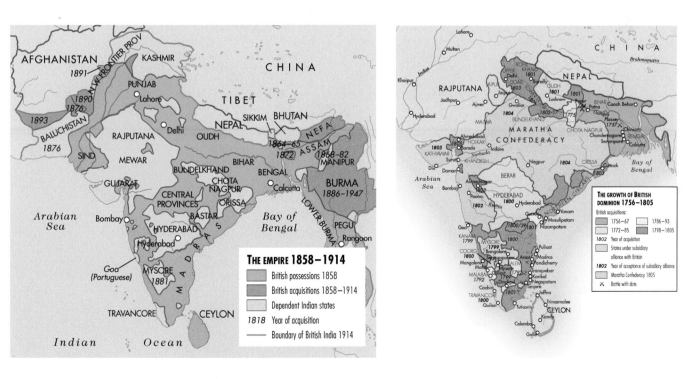

THE EMPIRE 1858–1914

- British possessions 1858
- British acquisitions 1858–1914
- Dependent Indian states
- *1818* Year of acquisition
- — Boundary of British India 1914

THE GROWTH OF BRITISH DOMINION 1756–1805

British acquisitions:
- 1756–67
- 1772–85
- 1786–93
- 1798–1805

1802 Year of acquisition

States under subsidiary alliance with Britain

1802 Year of acceptance of subsidiary alliance

Maratha Confederacy 1805

× Battle with date

49. Empires, Trade, and Migration
1880–1914

✳ ✳ ✳

The strengthening of European colonial rule across the world in the late 19th century was linked to a number of economic and political factors, including the need for raw materials to supply rapidly industrializing economies and the desire to find new markets for manufactured goods. At the same time, many Europeans left their native countries in search of a better life for themselves and their families. Around 30 million people left Europe between 1815 and 1914 bound for the United States. Later European settlers headed for South Africa and beyond, to Australia and New Zealand.

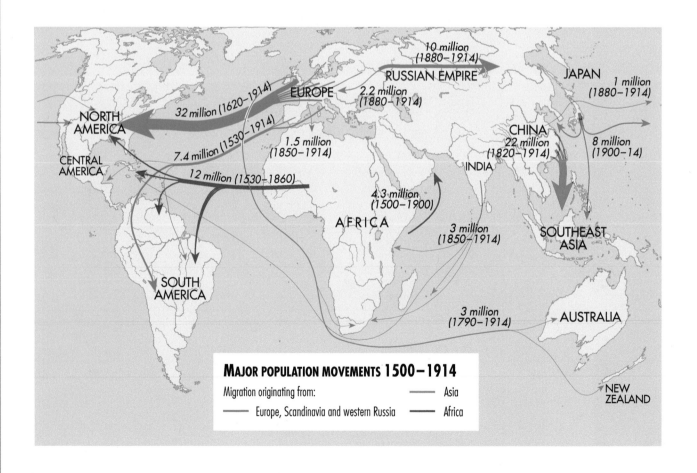

MAJOR POPULATION MOVEMENTS 1500–1914

Migration originating from:

— Europe, Scandinavia and western Russia

— Asia

— Africa

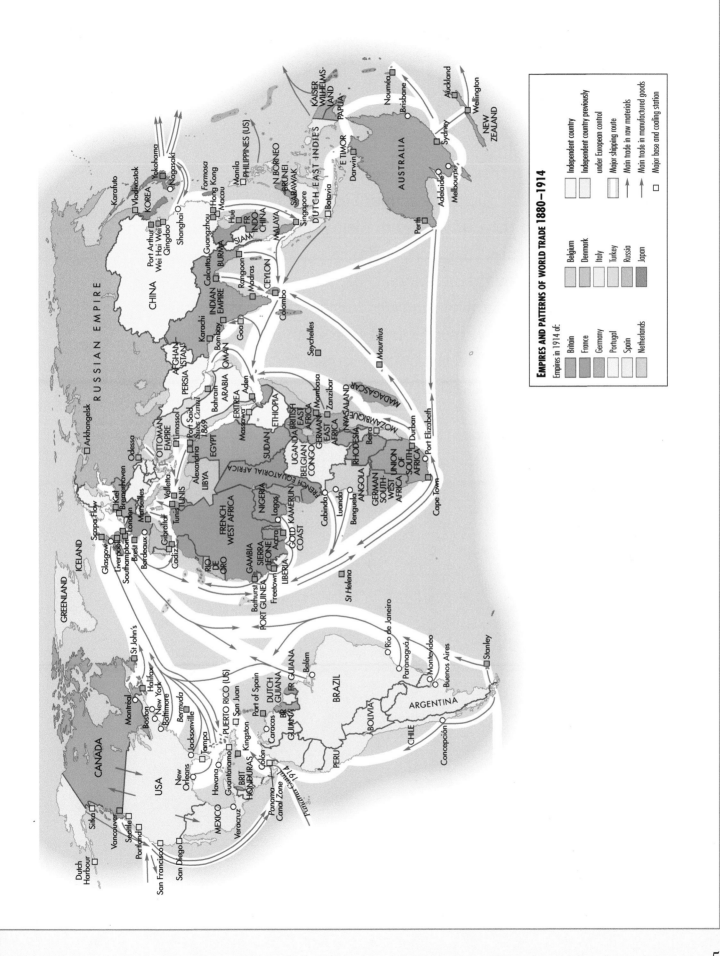

EMPIRES AND PATTERNS OF WORLD TRADE 1880–1914

Empires in 1914 of:

Britain	Belgium
France	Denmark
Germany	Italy
Portugal	Turkey
Spain	Russia
Netherlands	Japan

Independent country

Independent country previously under European control

Major shipping route

↑ Main trade in raw materials

↑ Main trade in manufactured goods

□ Major base and coaling station

GREENLAND

ICELAND

RUSSIAN EMPIRE

CANADA

USA

Dutch Harbour
Sitka
Vancouver
Seattle
Portland
San Francisco
San Diego
Portland
New Orleans
Tampa
Jacksonville
Baltimore
New York
Boston
Halifax
Montreal
St John's
Bermuda
Havana
Guantánamo
MEXICO
Veracruz
BRIT HONDURAS
Colón
Panama Canal Zone 1914
Kingston
PUERTO RICO (US)
San Juan
Caracas
Port of Spain
GUIANA
BR GUIANA
DUTCH GUIANA
FR GUIANA
Belém

PERU
BOLIVIA
CHILE
Concepción
BRAZIL
Rio de Janeiro
Paranaguá
ARGENTINA
Montevideo
Buenos Aires
Stanley

Glasgow
Liverpool
Southampton
Brest
Bordeaux
London
Bremerhaven
Kiel
Scapa Flow
Odessa
Marseilles
Gibraltar
Cadiz
OTTOMAN EMPIRE
Limassol
Port Said
Suez Canal 1869
Alexandria
EGYPT
LIBYA
TUNIS
Tunis
Valletta
Bizerta

FRENCH WEST AFRICA
RIO DE ORO
GAMBIA
Bathurst
PORT GUINEA
SIERRA LEONE
Freetown
LIBERIA
GOLD COAST
Accra
NIGERIA
Lagos
KAMERUN
FRENCH EQUATORIAL AFRICA
St Helena
Cabinda
Luanda
ANGOLA
Benguela
GERMAN SOUTH-WEST AFRICA
UNION OF SOUTH AFRICA
Cape Town
Port Elizabeth
Durban
BELGIAN CONGO
UGANDA
RHODESIA
NYASALAND
MOZAMBIQUE
Beira
GERMAN EAST AFRICA
BRITISH EAST AFRICA
Mombasa
Zanzibar
SUDAN
ETHIOPIA
ERITREA
Massawa
Aden
ARABIA
OMAN
Bahrain
PERSIA
AFGHANISTAN
Karachi
Bombay
Goa
INDIAN EMPIRE
Calcutta
Madras
Rangoon
BURMA
CEYLON
Colombo
Seychelles
Mauritius
MADAGASCAR

Arkhangelsk
Karafuto
Vladivostok
Yokohama
Nagasaki
KOREA
Port Arthur
Wei Hai Wei
Qingdao
Shanghai
CHINA
Guangzhou
Hong Kong
Macau
Hué
FR INDO-CHINA
SIAM
MALAYA
Singapore
Manila
PHILIPPINES (US)
N BORNEO
BRUNEI
SARAWAK
DUTCH EAST INDIES
Batavia
E TIMOR
KAISER WILHELMS-LAND
PAPUA
Darwin
AUSTRALIA
Perth
Adelaide
Melbourne
Sydney
Brisbane
Nouméa
Auckland
Wellington
NEW ZEALAND

50. Wars and Revolutions

1770–1913

✳ ✳ ✳

Military conflicts within Europe in this period were caused largely by the territorial ambitions of the French, the Russians, and the Prussians. Smaller conflicts arose as Belgium, Greece, Hungary, Italy, and, at the very end of the period, the Balkan states fought off colonial rule and established their independence. Many of the wars outside Europe were fought by European powers or by people of European origin. In Latin America, for example, there was a sequence of wars of liberation as the Spanish colonial elites staged successful revolutions against rule from Spain.

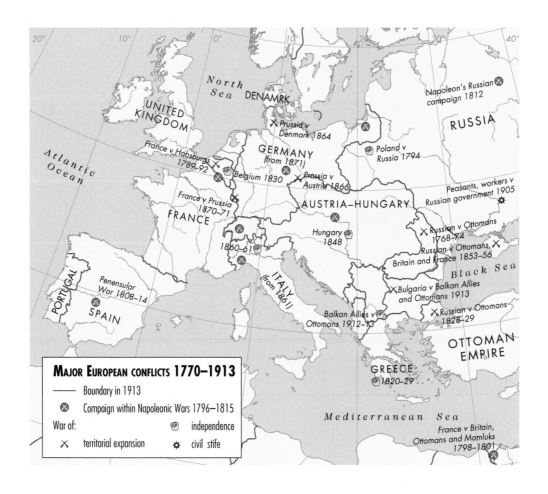

MAJOR EUROPEAN CONFLICTS **1770–1913**

—— Boundary in 1913

⊗ Compaign within Napoleonic Wars 1796–1815

War of:

✕ territorial expansion ✊ independence ✷ civil stife

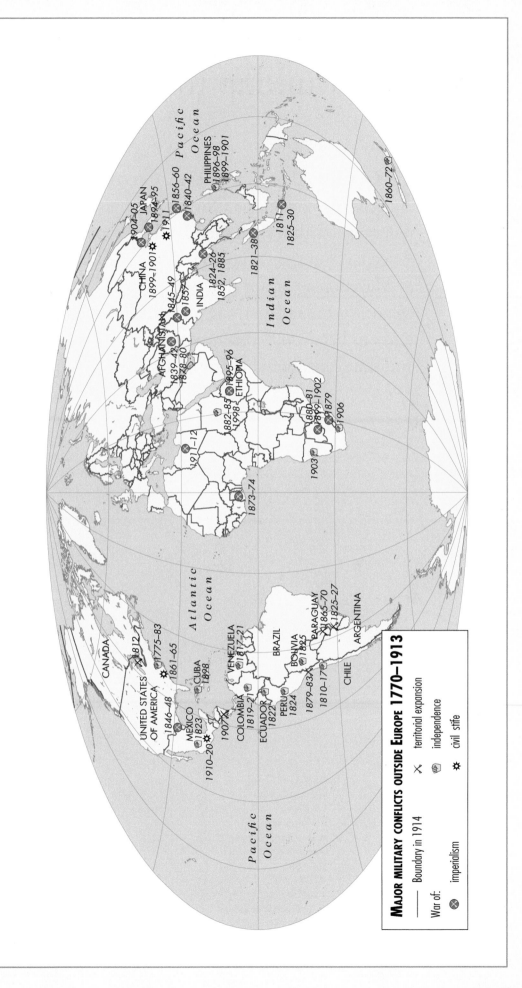

MAJOR MILITARY CONFLICTS OUTSIDE EUROPE 1770–1913

Boundary in 1914

War of:
⊗ imperialism

✕ territorial expansion

👊 independence

✿ civil strife

Pacific Ocean

Atlantic Ocean

Indian Ocean

Pacific Ocean

CANADA

UNITED STATES OF AMERICA
1775–83
1812
1861–65
1846–48

MEXICO
1823
1907
1910–20

CUBA
1898

COLOMBIA
1819–21

VENEZUELA
1817–21

ECUADOR
1822

PERU
1824

BOLIVIA
1810–17
1825

BRAZIL

PARAGUAY
1865–70
1825–27

CHILE
1879–83

ARGENTINA

JAPAN
1904–05
1894–95
1911

CHINA
1899–1901
1856–60
1840–42

PHILIPPINES
1896–98
1899–1901

AFGHANISTAN
1839–42
1878–80

INDIA
1845–49
1857
1824–26
1852, 1885

1821–38

1811
1825–30

1860–72

ETHIOPIA
1882–85
1998
1895–96

1880–81
1899–1902
1879
1906

1903

1873–74

1911–12

53

51. The Buildup to the First World War

✳ ✳ ✳

In October 1912 Montenegro, Greece, Serbia, and Bulgaria declared wars on the Ottoman Empire. As a result, the Ottomans relinquished almost all their lands in southeast Europe in 1913. A second war then erupted between Bulgaria and Serbia over territory in Macedonia—a war that Serbia won. These two Balkan Wars, in creating a militarily strong and ambitious Serbia, inflamed existing tensions between Serbia (supported by Russia) and Austria-Hungary and thus contributed to the outbreak of the First World War.

THE BALKAN WARS 1912–13

- – – Border of country or province 1912
- —— Border of country 1914
- ▢ Austro-Hungarian Empire 1878
- ▢ Administered by Austria–Hungary from 1878

Territory gaining independence from Ottoman Empire:
- ▢ 1830–1908
- ▢ 1912–13
- ▢ Ottoman Empire 1914

1878 Date of independence from Ottoman Empire

The system of alliances between the countries of Europe in 1914 ensured that when Austria threatened Serbia following the assassination of Archduke Ferdinand, all the major European powers rapidly became involved.

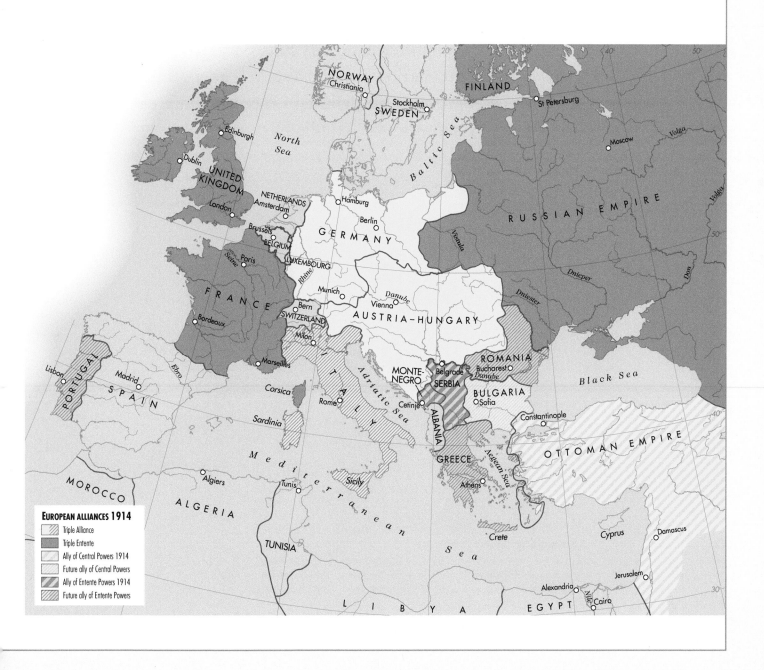

EUROPEAN ALLIANCES 1914
- Triple Alliance
- Triple Entente
- Ally of Central Powers 1914
- Future ally of Central Powers
- Ally of Entente Powers 1914
- Future ally of Entente Powers

52. Outcomes of the First World War

✳ ✳ ✳

As a result of the Paris Peace Conference of 1919, the Austro-Hungarian Empire was dismantled. Most of it was formed into small nation-states. In the south, however, several ethnically distinct regions were amalgamated with previously independent states to form Yugoslavia. Germany lost territory in the east to the re-created Poland, while a demilitarized area was established along German's border with France. The newly formed Union of Soviet Socialist Republics, threatened by anti-revolutionary forces, was in no position to resist moves to carve up territory on its western borders. The Treaty of Sévres (1920) divided the defeated Ottoman Empire into British and French mandates in the Middle East. ◆

THE DIVISION OF THE OTTOMAN EMPIRE

▨ Republic of Turkey after Treaty of Lausanne 1923	▨ French mandate	▨ British influence
— Boundary of Turkey after Treaty of Sèvres 1920	▢ British mandate	1920 Date of mandate
— Boundary of spheres of influence in Turkey 1920–22	▨ British colony	**1922** Date of independence

TREATY SETTLEMENTS IN EUROPE 1919–23

- Boundary 1923
- Pre-war boundary
- Territory administered by League of Nations
- //// Demilitarized zone
- **1918** Date of independence

TREATIES BETWEEN ENTENTE POWERS AND DEFEATED COUNTRIES:

Treaty of Versailles 28 June 1919 – Entente Powers (excluding USA) and Germany
Treaty of Saint-Germain 10 September 1919 – Entente Powers and Austria
Treaty of Neuilly 24 November 1919 – Entente Powers and Bulgaria
Treaty of Trianon 4 June 1920 – Entente Powers and Hungary
Treaty of Sèvres 10 August 1920 – Entente Powers (excluding USA and USSR)
and Turkey (Sultanate of), superseded by:
Treaty of Lausanne 24 July 1923 with Turkish Republic
Treaty of Berlin 2 July 1921 – USA and Germany

53. Revolution and Civil War in Russia

* * *

The Russian Revolution—one of the formative events of the 20th century—was precipitated by pressures arising from the hardships experienced during the First World War. After sweeping away the provisional government in November 1917, the Bolsheviks faced widespread opposition both within and outside Russia. The Treaty of Brest-Litovsk in March 1918 ended the war with Germany but led to a civil war in which the Entente Powers initially supported the "Whites" (anti-Bolsheviks) against the "Reds" (the Bolsheviks).

REVOLUTION AND CIVIL WAR IN RUSSIA

- – – – Boundary of the Russian Empire 1914
- ──── German occupation line March 1918
- ✺ Centre of great Bolshevik activity
- ➡ White Russian and interventionist attacks

Interventionists:
- **C** Canadian
- **F** French
- **G** Greek
- **B** British
- **US** American

- ──── Boundary of area controlled by Bolsheviks August 1918
- Area controlled by Bolsheviks October 1919
- Polish advance into Russia May 1920
- Russian advance into Poland August 1920
- – – – USSR–Polish boundary established October 1920 by Treaty of Riga
- ──── Other international boundaries 1922
- Areas lost to Russia 1914–21
- Soviet Union 1922

53. Revolution and Civil War in Russia

✳ ✳ ✳

The First World War and civil war had a devastating effect on Russia's industrial output, reducing it by 1920 to one-fifth of its 1913 level. Manufacturing had recovered by 1928 when the First Five-Year Plan was launched.

THE SOVIET UNION 1928–39

○ Town founded before 1917 (1939 name)
● Town founded 1917–39 (1939 names)

Symbols in ■ : developed before 1928
Symbols in ■ : developed 1928–39

▣ ▣ Coal mining and lignite mining
▢ ▢ Gold mining
▣ ▣ Iron mining
△ △ Copper mining

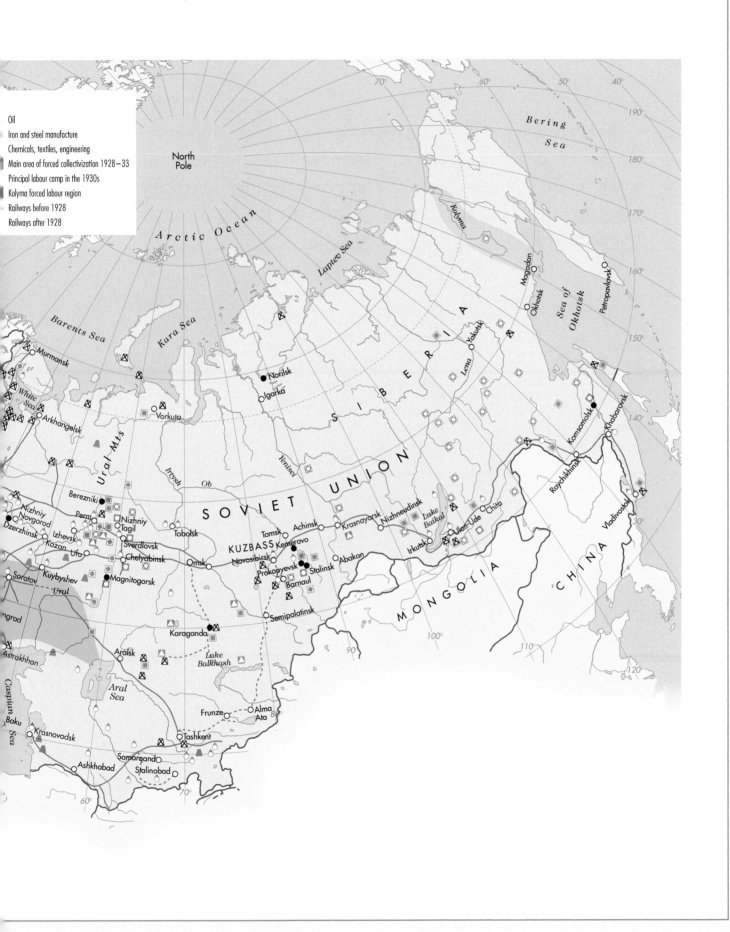

Oil
Iron and steel manufacture
Chemicals, textiles, engineering
Main area of forced collectivization 1928–33
Principal labour camp in the 1930s
Kolyma forced labour region
Railways before 1928
Railways after 1928

North
Pole

*Bering
Sea*

190°

180°

170°

Arctic Ocean

160°

Kolyma

Laptev Sea

Magadan

Okhotsk

150°

*Sea of
Okhotsk*

Petropavlovsk

Barents Sea

Kara Sea

Murmansk

140°

*White
Sea*

Norilsk

Arkhangelsk

Olgarka

S I B E R I A

Yakutsk

Khabarovsk

Komsomolsk

Lena

Vorkuta

Ural Mts

Irtysh

Ob

Yenisei

S O V I E T   U N I O N

Raychikhinsk

Bere15zniki

Perm

Nizhniy
Novgorod

Nizhniy
Tagil

Tobolsk

Tomsk

Achinsk

Krasnayarsk

Nizhneudinsk

*Lake
Baikal*

Chita

Vladivostok

30°

Dzerzhinsk

Izhevsk

Sverdlovsk

KUZBASS

Kemerovo

Ulan-Ude

Kazan

Ufa

Chelyabinsk

Novosibirsk

Irkutsk

Saratov

Kuybyshev

Omsk

Prokopyevsk

Stalinsk

Abakan

CHINA

Magnitogorsk

Barnaul

MONGOLIA

Ural

Semipalatinsk

110°

ngrad

120°

Astrakhhan

Karaganda

100°

*Caspian
Sea*

Aralsk

*Lake
Balkhash*

90°

Baku

Krasnovodsk

Frunze

Alma
Ata

Ashkhabad

Samargand

Tashkent

Stalinobad

60°

70°

61

54. The Great Depression

✳ ✳ ✳

Every country in Europe experienced a drop in industrial production during the Depression, with the northeast being worst hit. In Germany dissatisfaction with the high unemployment rate provided a platform on which Hitler and the Nazi Party came to power in 1933.

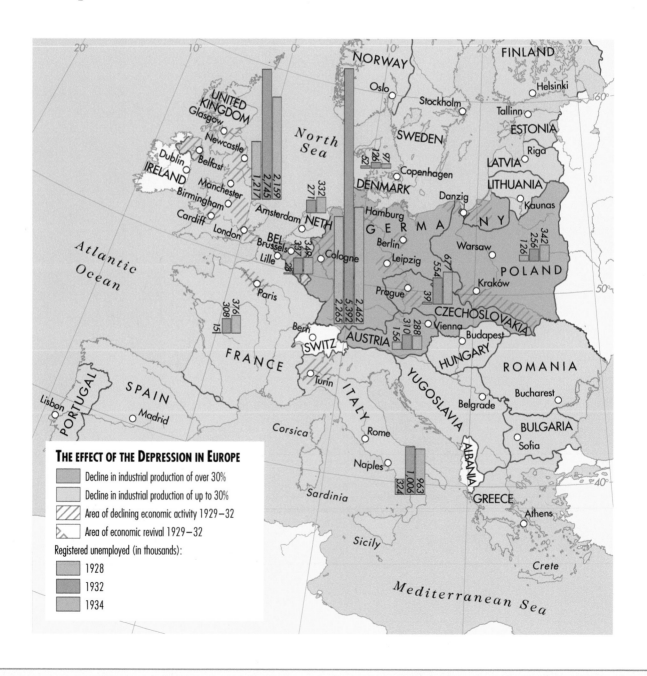

THE EFFECT OF THE DEPRESSION IN EUROPE

- Decline in industrial production of over 30%
- Decline in industrial production of up to 30%
- Area of declining economic activity 1929–32
- Area of economic revival 1929–32

Registered unemployed (in thousands):
- 1928
- 1932
- 1934

Countries around the world that supplied raw materials for the factories of industrialized nations were hit by the drop in production during the Depression. Chile, for example, saw its exports drop by over 80 percent, and India and Brazil suffered a fall of over 60 percent.

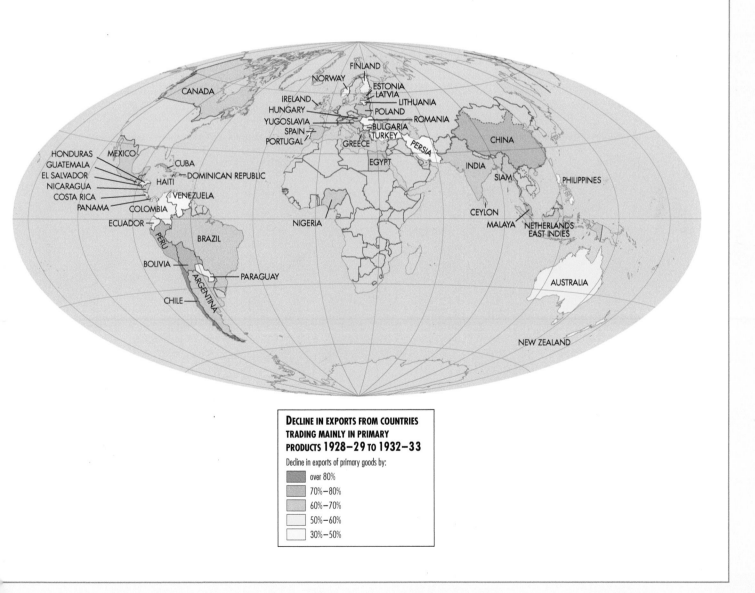

DECLINE IN EXPORTS FROM COUNTRIES TRADING MAINLY IN PRIMARY PRODUCTS 1928–29 TO 1932–33

Decline in exports of primary goods by:

	over 80%
	70%–80%
	60%–70%
	50%–60%
	30%–50%

55. The Rise of Fascism

1922–1939

✳ ✳ ✳

In the years between the two world wars, a political and socio-cultural phenomenon known as Fascism arose in Europe. Its exact form varied from country to country, but it was most commonly characterized by chauvinistic nationalism coupled with expansionist tendencies, anti-Communism, and a ruthless repression of all groups presumed dissident, a mass party with a charismatic leader who rose to power through legitimate elections, and a dependence on alliances with industrial, agrarian, military, and bureaucratic allies.

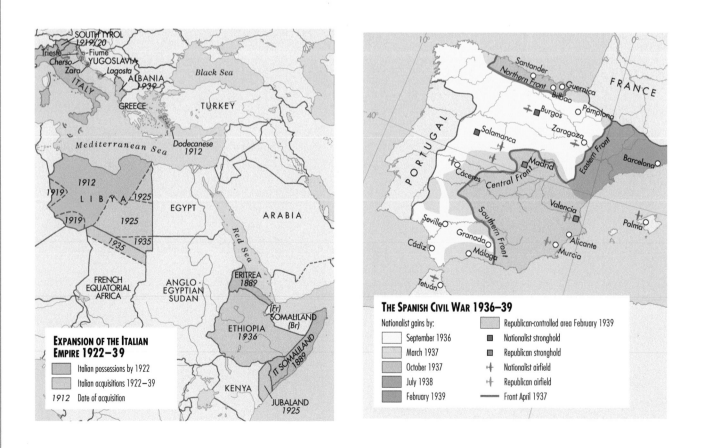

EXPANSION OF THE ITALIAN EMPIRE 1922–39

Italian possessions by 1922
Italian acquisitions 1922–39
1912 Date of acquisition

THE SPANISH CIVIL WAR 1936–39

Nationalist gains by:
September 1936
March 1937
October 1937
July 1938
February 1939

Republican-controlled area February 1939
■ Nationalist stronghold
■ Republican stronghold
✠ Nationalist airfield
✠ Republican airfield
— Front April 1937

EXPANSION OF NAZI GERMANY 1933–39

- Germany 1933
- Saar-region, incorporated 1935
- Rhineland demilitarized zone, occupied 1936

Territory annexed by Germany:
- on 13 March 1938
- on 1 October 1938
- in March 1939
- by 31 December 1939

SWEDEN

DENMARK

Copenhagen

Baltic Sea

LATVIA

Riga

LITHUANIA

Kaunas

Memel Territory
23 March 1939

Königsberg

Danzig
19 Sept 1939

EAST PRUSSIA

Amsterdam

NETHERLANDS

Hamburg

Weser

Elbe

Berlin

Hanover

G E R M A N Y

Poznań

Vistula

Bug

Warsaw

RUSSIAN OCCUPATION

17 Sept 1939

Brussels

BELGIUM

Cologne

Rhine

Leipzig

P O L A N D

Oder

Frankfurt

LUX

SAAR

Saarbrücken

Paris

Seine

Nuremberg

Stuttgart

SUDETEN-LAND

Prague

PROTECTORATE OF BOHEMIA–MORAVIA
16 March 1939

Kraków

GENERAL GOVERNMENT OF POLAND
12 Oct 1939

Lvov

Freiburg

Rhine

FRANCE

Munich

Danube

PROTECTORATE OF SLOVAKIA
23 March 1939

to Hungary 1938

to Hungary
23 March 1939

Saône

Bern

Geneva

SWITZERLAND

Innsbruck

Salzburg

AUSTRIA

Vienna

Budapest

HUNGARY

Lyons

Rhône

Trent

Venice

Trieste

ROMANIA

ITALY

Po

YUGOSLAVIA

56. The Second World War in Europe

✳ ✳ ✳

Nazi Germany retained control in its conquered territories by installing puppet governments in the Balkans and its own administrations in Poland and the western Soviet Union. Italian and German troops jointly occupied Greece until the Italian surrender in 1943. Concentration and death camps were constructed, to which "undesirables," and in particular Jews, were transported from across Europe.

GERMANY'S "NEW ORDER" IN EUROPE NOVEMBER 1942

- German Reich
- Territory under German administration
- Territory under German occupation
- Italy and annexed/administered territories
- Countries co-operating with Axis
- Countries occupied by Axis
- Vichy-governed France
- Unconquered territory of USSR
- Territory of Allied Powers
- Neutral countries
- —— International boundary
- —— German border 1937
- ⊠ Concentration camp
- ⊠ Major death camp

During the final months of the war a race took place between the Western Allies and the Soviet Union for control of German territory. The two armies eventually met west of the German capital Berlin and the Austrian capital of Vienna. They agreed to divide these symbolically important cities into zones of occupation.

CENTRAL EUROPE 1945

- Future Soviet bloc countries
- Western allies and countries liberated by them
- Neutral countries
- Germany
- Areas controlled by Western allies
- Areas controlled by USSR
- Meeting of Soviet and Western forces
- International boundary 1945
- Functioning boundary of 1945
- German boundary at end of 1939
- City divided into four occupation zones

57. The Breakdown of Empires

1939–2008

❋ ❋ ❋

Before the Second World War the European colonial empires seemed largely secure despite independence movements in India and French Indochina. Yet within twenty years of the war's end most colonies had become independent.

DECOLONIZATION FROM 1945

- Independence gained 1945–65
- Independence gained 1966–08
- Colonies/dependencies 2008

1970 Date of independence

Countries administered by:

- Australia
- France
- New Zealand
- Portugal
- Spain
- Britain
- United States
- Commonwealth of USA

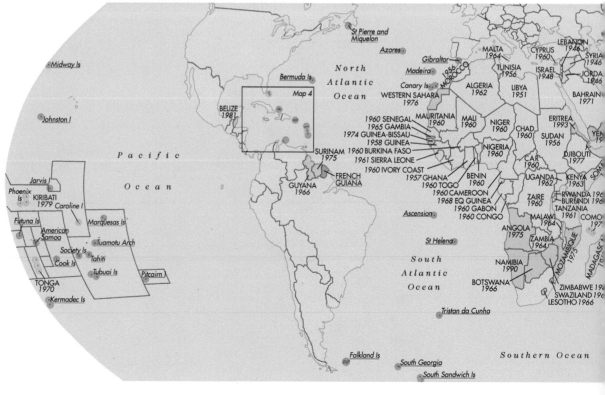

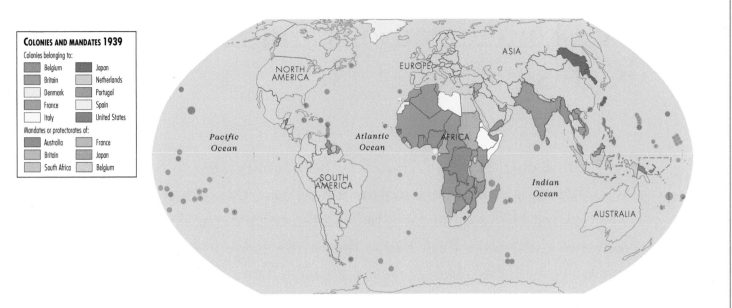

COLONIES AND MANDATES 1939

Colonies belonging to:

- Belgium
- Britain
- Denmark
- France
- Italy
- Japan
- Netherlands
- Portugal
- Spain
- United States

Mandates or protectorates of:

- Australia
- Britain
- South Africa
- France
- Japan
- Belgium

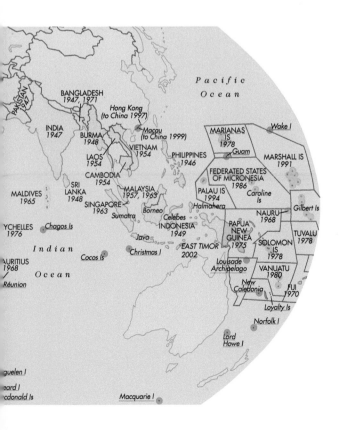

PAKISTAN
1947

BANGLADESH
1947, 1971

Hong Kong
(to China 1997)

INDIA
1947

BURMA
1948

Macau
(to China 1999)

VIETNAM
1954

LAOS
1954

CAMBODIA
1954

SRI
LANKA
1948

MALDIVES
1965

MALAYSIA
1957, 1963

SINGAPORE
1963

Sumatra

Borneo

Celebes

Halmahera

SEYCHELLES
1976

Chagos Is

Java

INDONESIA
1949

Christmas I

Cocos Is

EAST TIMOR
2002

MAURITIUS
1968

Réunion

Indian

Ocean

Louisade
Archipelago

New
Caledonia

Loyalty Is

Norfolk I

Lord
Howe I

Kerguelen I

Heard I

Macdonald Is

Macquarie I

Pacific
Ocean

MARIANAS
IS
1978

Wake I

Guam

MARSHALL IS
1991

PHILIPPINES
1946

FEDERATED STATES
OF MICRONESIA
1986

PALAU IS
1994

Caroline
Is

Gilbert Is

NAURU
1968

PAPUA
NEW
GUINEA
1975

SOLOMON
IS
1978

TUVALU
1978

VANUATU
1980

FIJI
1970

58. The United Nations and Human Rights

✳ ✳ ✳

The first purpose of the United Nations, enunciated in the UN Charter, is to maintain international peace and security. In 1948 the first UN ground force policed the truce in the Middle East, though it was not until 1956 that a full-fledged peacekeeping force was established. Religious and ethnic differences have led to intense conflict in many regions of the world since 1945, although issues such as inequality of social status, income, and land distribution are frequently strong contributing factors. ⟡

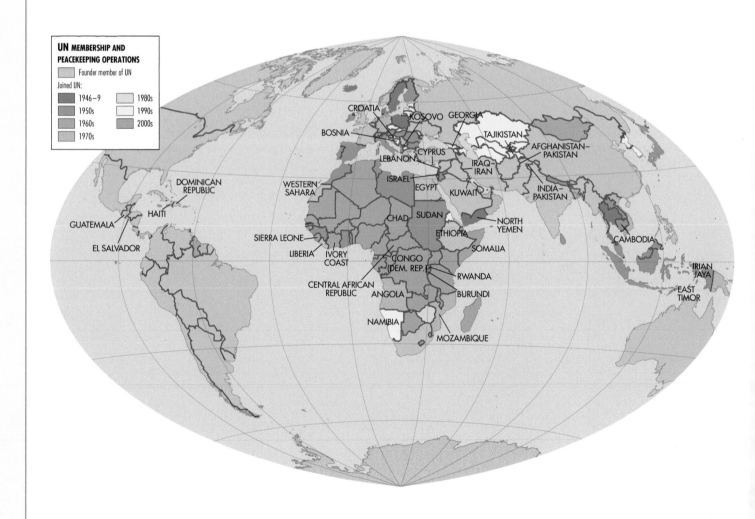

UN MEMBERSHIP AND PEACEKEEPING OPERATIONS

Founder member of UN

Joined UN:
- 1946–9
- 1950s
- 1960s
- 1970s
- 1980s
- 1990s
- 2000s

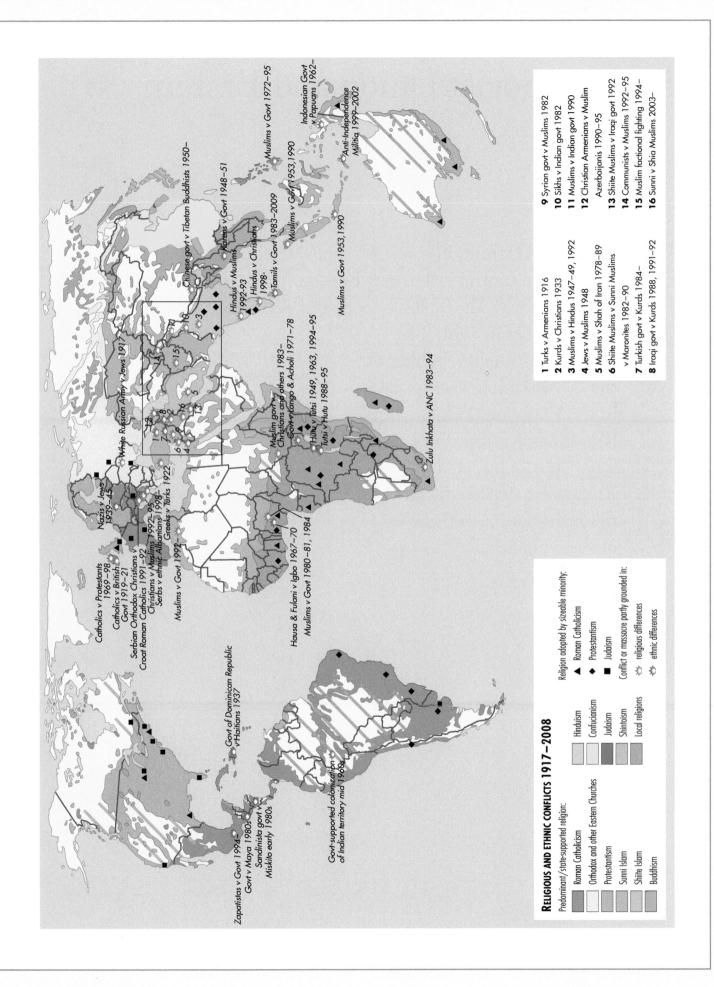

RELIGIOUS AND ETHNIC CONFLICTS 1917–2008

Predominant/state-supported religion:

- Roman Catholicism
- Orthodox and other Eastern Churches
- Protestantism
- Sunni Islam
- Shiite Islam
- Buddhism
- Hinduism
- Confucianism
- Judaism
- Shintoism
- Local religions

Religion adopted by sizeable minority:

- ▲ Roman Catholicism
- ◆ Protestantism
- ■ Judaism

Conflict or massacre partly grounded in:
- ⚔ religious differences
- ⚔ ethnic differences

1 Turks v Armenians 1916
2 Kurds v Christians 1933
3 Muslims v Hindus 1947–49, 1992
4 Jews v Muslims 1948
5 Muslims v Shah of Iran 1978–89
6 Shiite Muslims v Sunni Muslims v Maronites 1982–90
7 Turkish govt v Kurds 1984–
8 Iraqi govt v Kurds 1988, 1991–92
9 Syrian govt v Muslims 1982
10 Sikhs v Indian govt 1982
11 Muslims v Indian govt 1990
12 Christian Armenians v Muslim Azerbaijanis 1990–95
13 Shiite Muslims v Iraqi govt 1992
14 Communists v Muslims 1992–95
15 Muslim factional fighting 1994–
16 Sunni v Shia Muslims 2003–

Chinese govt v Tibetan Buddhists 1950–
Karens v Govt 1948–51
Muslims v Govt 1972–95
Hindus v Muslims 1992–93
Hindus v Christians 1998–
Tamils v Govt 1983–2009
Muslims v Govt 1953, 1990
Muslims v Govt 1953, 1990
Indonesian Govt v Papuans 1962–
Anti-independence Militia 1999–2002

White Russian Army v Jews 1917
Nazis v Jews 1939–45
Catholics v Protestants 1969–98
Catholics v British Govt 1919–21
Serbian Orthodox Christians v Croat Roman Catholics 1991–92
Christians v Muslims 1992–95
Serbs v ethnic Albanians 1998–
Muslims v Govt 1992–
Greeks v Turks 1922

Muslim govt v Christians and others 1983–
Govt v Lango & Acholi 1971–78
Hutu v Tutsi 1949, 1963, 1994–95
Tutsi v Hutu 1988–95
Hausa & Fulani v Igbo 1967–70
Muslims v Govt 1980–81, 1984
Zulu Inkhata v ANC 1983–94

Zapatistas v Govt 1994–
Govt v Maya 1980s
Sandinista govt v Miskito early 1980s
Govt of Dominican Republic v Haitians 1937
Govt-supported colonization of Indian territory mid 1960s

59. The Soviet Union and Eastern Europe

1945–1989

✳ ✳ ✳

By 1948 Communist parties, supported by the Soviet Union, were in control in Eastern Europe. Yugoslavia refused to align itself with the Soviet Union, and Albania broke its economic ties in 1961. The fifteen constituent republics of the Soviet Union were formed in the 1920s and 1930s, largely along ethnic lines. They were dominated by the Russian Federation, by far the largest and wealthiest of the republics. ✦

COMMUNIST EASTERN EUROPE 1945–89

Territory annexed by Soviet Union 1939–40
Territory annexed by Soviet Union 1945–47
Independent communist state after 1948
Allied with China after 1961
Territory under Russian occupation 1945
Iron Curtain

Soviet intervention 1956
Soviet intervention 1968
Strong Soviet pressure 1956, 1980
COMECON member 1949–91
Warsaw Pact member 1955–91
City divided into zones of occupation

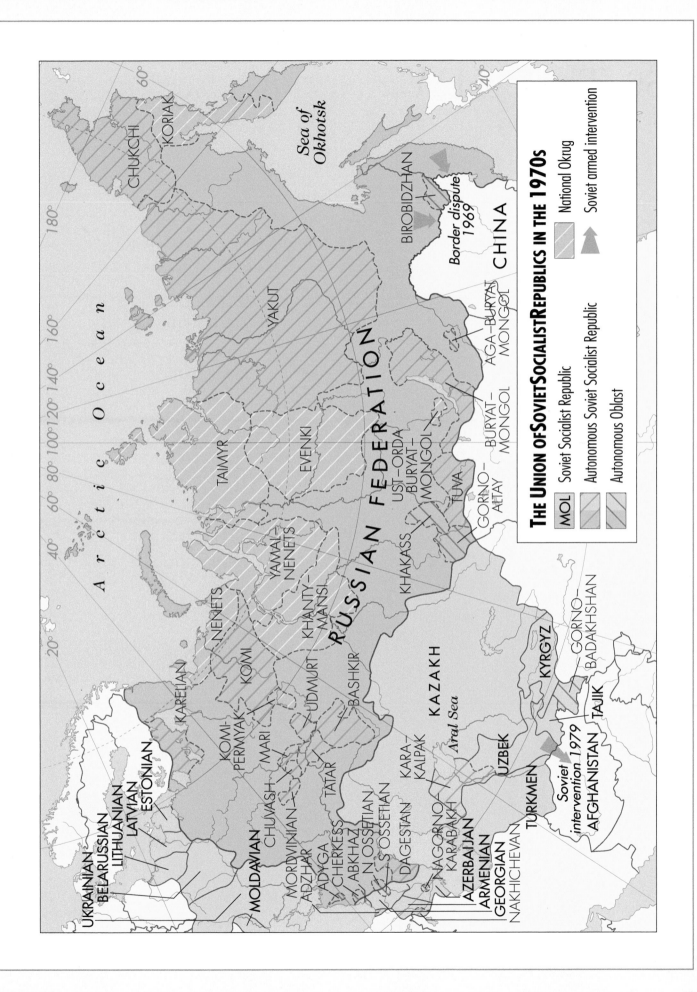

THE UNION OF SOVIET SOCIALIST REPUBLICS IN THE 1970s

MOL		Soviet Socialist Republic
		Autonomous Soviet Socialist Republic
		Autonomous Oblast
		National Okrug
		Soviet armed intervention

RUSSIAN FEDERATION

Arctic Ocean

Sea of Okhotsk

CHINA

Border dispute 1969

Soviet intervention 1979

CHUKCHI
KORIAK
YAKUT
BIROBIDZHAN
TAIMYR
EVENKI
UST-ORDA BURYAT-MONGOL
AGA-BURYAT MONGOL
BURYAT-MONGOL
TUVA
GORNO-ALTAY
KHAKASS
YAMAL-NENETS
KHANTY-MANSI
NENETS
KOMI
KOMI-PERMYAK
MARI
UDMURT
BASHKIR
CHUVASH
MORDVINIAN
TATAR
KARELIAN
ESTONIAN
LATVIAN
LITHUANIAN
BELARUSSIAN
UKRAINIAN
MOLDAVIAN
ADZHAR
ADYGA
CHERKESS
ABKHAZ
N.OSSETIAN
S.OSSETIAN
DAGESTAN
NAGORNO-KARABAKH
NAKHICHEVAN
GEORGIAN
ARMENIAN
AZERBAIJAN
KARA-KALPAK
KAZAKH
Aral Sea
UZBEK
TURKMEN
AFGHANISTAN
TAJIK
GORNO-BADAKHSHAN
KYRGYZ

60. The Cold War

1947–1991

* * *

The Cold War was a period of political and economic confrontation between the two superpowers and their allies. The area of highest tension was along the "Iron Curtain" that divided Western and Eastern Europe, but the two sides' opposition was played out in conflicts all over the world, most notably in Korea. In 1962 U.S. reconnaissance flights detected evidence that the Soviet Union was building nuclear missile bases on Cuba within range of the U.S. mainland. A U.S. naval blockade, and a tense period during which nuclear war appeared likely, eventually resulted in the USSR agreeing to dismantle the nuclear bases. Vietnam's struggle for independence from the French resulted, in 1954, in the division of the country into communist North Vietnam and U.S.-backed South Vietnam. North Vietnam attempted to overthrow the southern regime and reunify the country. The United States, anxious to prevent the spread of Communism, became militarily involved in the 1960s but was eventually defeated by the Vietcong's guerrilla tactics.

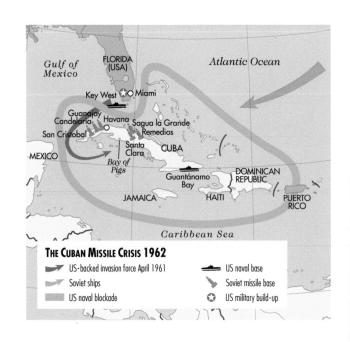

THE CUBAN MISSILE CRISIS 1962

- US-backed invasion force April 1961
- Soviet ships
- US naval blockade
- US naval base
- Soviet missile base
- US military build-up

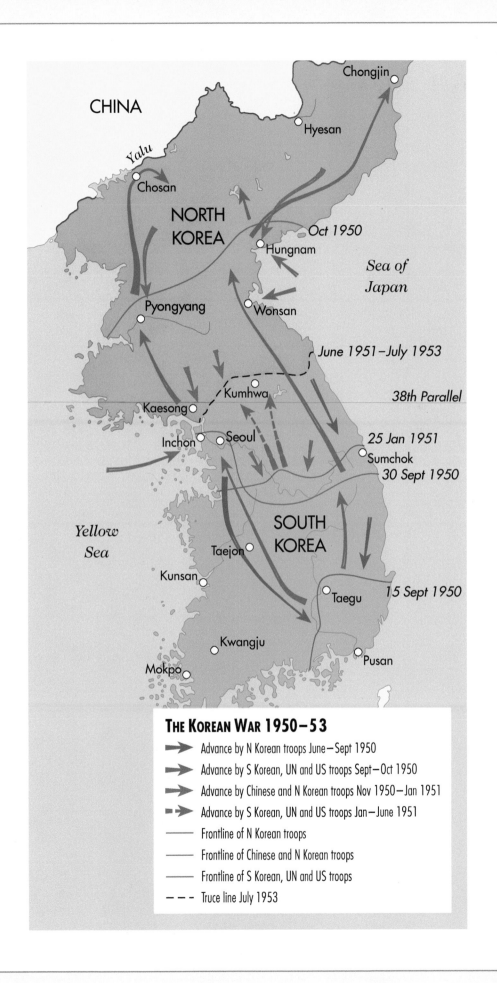

CHINA

Chongjin

Hyesan

Yalu

Chosan

NORTH KOREA

Oct 1950

Hungnam

Sea of Japan

Wonsan

Pyongyang

June 1951–July 1953

Kumhwa

38th Parallel

Kaesong

25 Jan 1951

Inchon   Seoul

Sumchok

30 Sept 1950

Yellow Sea

SOUTH KOREA

Taejon

Kunsan

Taegu   *15 Sept 1950*

Kwangju

Mokpo   Pusan

THE KOREAN WAR 1950–53

➡ Advance by N Korean troops June–Sept 1950

➡ Advance by S Korean, UN and US troops Sept–Oct 1950

➡ Advance by Chinese and N Korean troops Nov 1950–Jan 1951

➡ Advance by S Korean, UN and US troops Jan–June 1951

— Frontline of N Korean troops

— Frontline of Chinese and N Korean troops

— Frontline of S Korean, UN and US troops

--- Truce line July 1953

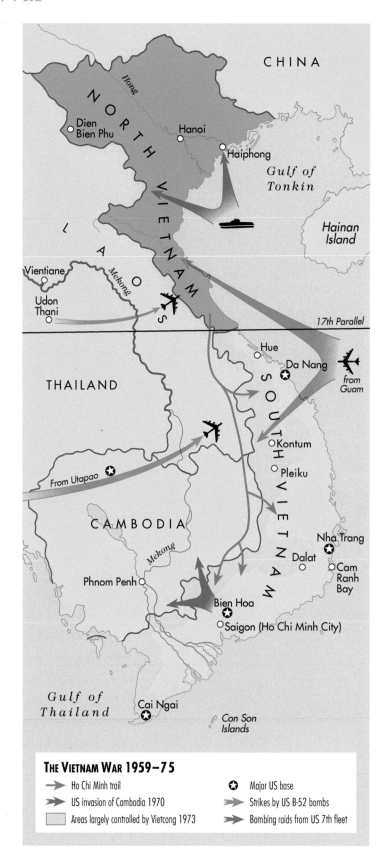

CHINA

Hong

Dien Bien Phu

Hanoi

Haiphong

Gulf of Tonkin

NORTH VIETNAM

Hainan Island

Vientiane

Mekong

LAOS

Udon Thani

17th Parallel

THAILAND

Hue

Da Nang

from Guam

Kontum

Pleiku

From Utapao

CAMBODIA

Mekong

SOUTH VIETNAM

Nha Trang

Dalat

Cam Ranh Bay

Phnom Penh

Bien Hoa

Saigon (Ho Chi Minh City)

Gulf of Thailand

Cai Ngai

Con Son Islands

THE VIETNAM WAR 1959–75

→ Ho Chi Minh trail

→ US invasion of Cambodia 1970

Areas largely controlled by Vietcong 1973

✪ Major US base

⇒ Strikes by US B-52 bombs

⇒ Bombing raids from US 7th fleet

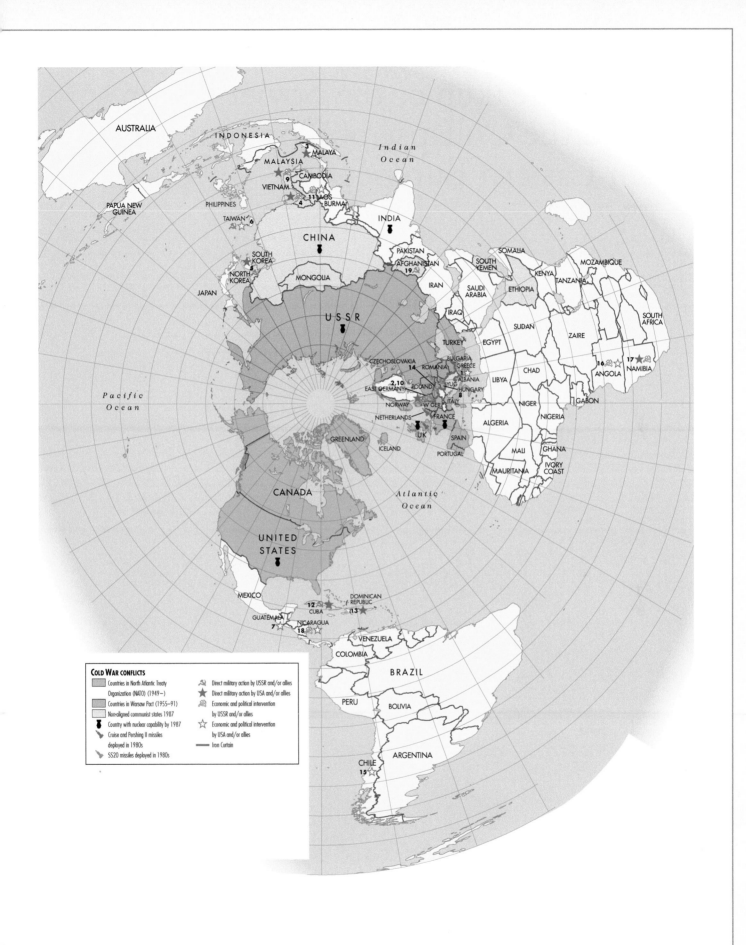

COLD WAR CONFLICTS

Countries in North Atlantic Treaty Organization (NATO) (1949–)

Countries in Warsaw Pact (1955–91)

Non-aligned communist states 1987

Country with nuclear capability by 1987

Cruise and Pershing II missiles deployed in 1980s

SS20 missiles deployed in 1980s

Direct military action by USSR and/or allies

Direct military action by USA and/or allies

Economic and political intervention by USSR and/or allies

Economic and political intervention by USA and/or allies

Iron Curtain

AUSTRALIA

INDONESIA

Indian Ocean

MALAYSIA · MALAYA · 3

VIETNAM · 9 · CAMBODIA

PAPUA NEW GUINEA

PHILIPPINES

BURMA · LAOS · 11 · 4

TAIWAN · 6

INDIA

CHINA

PAKISTAN

AFGHANISTAN · 19

SOMALIA

SOUTH YEMEN

MOZAMBIQUE

SOUTH KOREA · 5

NORTH KOREA

JAPAN

MONGOLIA

IRAN

SAUDI ARABIA

KENYA

ETHIOPIA

TANZANIA

SOUTH AFRICA

USSR

IRAQ

SUDAN

ZAIRE

Pacific Ocean

TURKEY

EGYPT

CZECHOSLOVAKIA · 14

BULGARIA · GREECE

ROMANIA · 1 · ALBANIA

16 · 17 · NAMIBIA

ANGOLA

2,10

EAST GERMANY · POLAND · YUG · HUNGARY · 8

LIBYA

CHAD

NORWAY · ITALY

W GER

NETHERLANDS · FRANCE

NIGER

ALGERIA

NIGERIA

GREENLAND

UK

SPAIN

ICELAND

MALI

GHANA

GABON

PORTUGAL

MAURITANIA

IVORY COAST

CANADA

Atlantic Ocean

UNITED STATES

MEXICO

DOMINICAN REPUBLIC

12 · CUBA

13

GUATEMALA · 7 · NICARAGUA · 18

VENEZUELA

COLOMBIA

BRAZIL

PERU

BOLIVIA

CHILE · 15

ARGENTINA

61. The Breakup of the Soviet Union and the Collapse of Communism in Eastern Europe

1947–1991

✳ ✳ ✳

The Soviet Union was formally abolished in December 1991. The collapse of the Communist regimes of Eastern Europe occurred between 1989 and 1990. With the exception of Yugoslavia and Romania, the "peoples' revolutions" in the former Warsaw Pact countries were carried off relatively peaceably.

THE TRANSITION FROM COMMUNISM TO DEMOCRACY FROM 1989

Location of main civil unrest

Sept 1989: East Germans allowed to cross from Hungary to Austria
Oct 1989: Demonstrations in Leipzig; Honecker resigns
Nov 1989: Berlin Wall brought down
March 1990: Multiparty elections
Oct 1990: German reunification

1985 onwards: Solidarity leads opposition to communism
June 1989: Elections held; communists defeated
Sept 1989: Solidarity forms government
May 1990: First multiparty elections; Solidarity wins

May 1988: Kadar replaced as party leader
Nov 1988: Alliance of Free Democrats formed
Sept 1989: Hungary lifts travel restrictions on East Germans
Mar/Apr 1990: Multiparty elections; Democratic Forum wins

Nov 1989: Mass demonstrations in Prague; opposition coalition formed
Dec 1989: Non-communist government formed; Havel elected president
June 1990: Multiparty elections
Jan 1993: State splits into Czech Republic and Slovakia

15–17 Dec 1989: Troops fire on demonstrators in Timisoara, killing 100 people
22 Dec 1989: Popular uprising against Ceausescu leads to his execution
May 1990: Elections won by ex-communist NSF but opposition disputes fairness
Sept 1992: First multiparty general election
Nov 1996: Elections won by opposition; first non-communist government

Apr 1990: Multiparty elections
June 1991: Declaration of independence; Yugoslavia puts up limited opposition

May 1990: Multiparty elections; Tudjman elected president
June 1991: Declaration of independence;
July 1991–Jan 1992: Fighting in Serb areas of Croatia

Dec 1990: Multiparty elections
Apr 1992: Fighting begins
Dec 1995: Dayton Peace Agreement divides Bosnia-Herzegovina in two

May 1989: Milosovic elected president of Serbia
1990: Multiparty elections in Serbia and Montenegro
1992: Referendum in Montenegro affirms support for Federal Republic of Yugoslavia
2006 Montenegro becomes independent state
1999: War breaks out in Serbia
2008: Kosovo declares independence

Nov 1989: Zhivkov resigns in Sofia; United
Dec 1989: Demonstration in Sofia; former Democratic Front formed
June 1990: Multiparty elections; former communists win
Oct 1991: Legislative elections; UDF beats former communists

Dec 1990: Multiparty elections
Sept 1991: Declaration of independence

Dec 1990: Pro-democracy demonstrations; Democratic Party formed
March 1991: Multiparty elections; Communist Party wins

UNITED KINGDOM
WEST GERMANY
EAST GERMANY
Berlin
Leipzig
GERMANY
Gdansk
POLAND
Warsaw
UNION OF SOVIET SOCIALIST REPUBLICS (until December 1991)
Prague
CZECH REPUBLIC
CZECHOSLOVAKIA
SLOVAKIA
Bratislava
FRANCE
SWITZERLAND
AUSTRIA
Budapest
HUNGARY
SLOVENIA
CROATIA
VOJVO-DINA
Timisoara
ROMANIA
Bucharest
BOSNIA-HERZEGOVINA
Belgrade
YUGOSLAVIA
SERBIA
ITALY
MONTE NEGRO
KOSOVO
Sofia
BULGARIA
MACEDONIA
Tirana
ALBANIA
GREECE
TURKEY

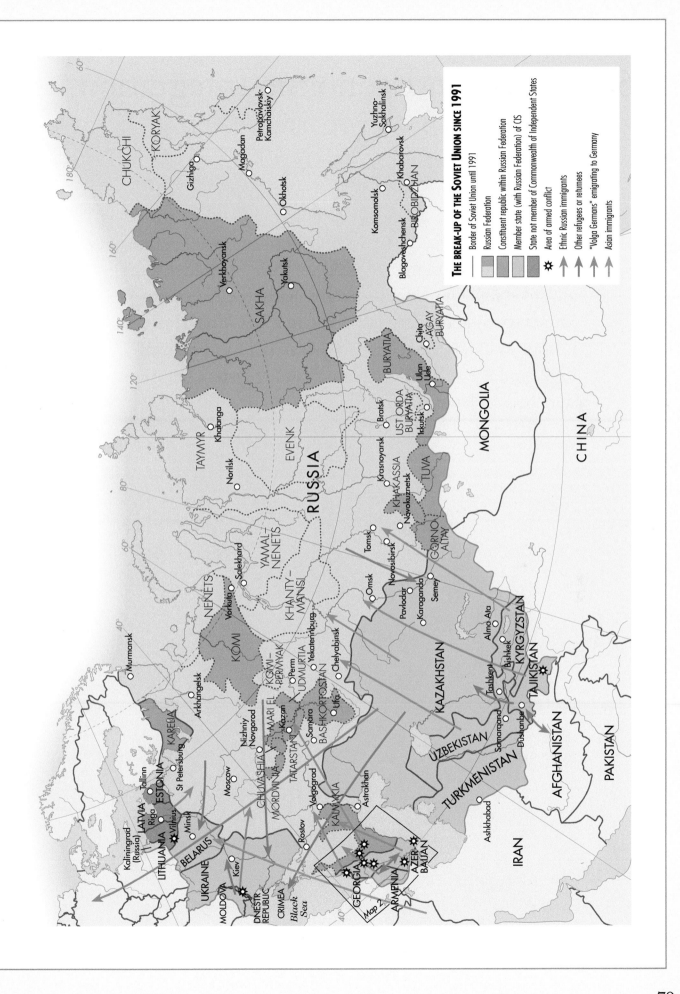

THE BREAK-UP OF THE SOVIET UNION SINCE 1991

- Border of Soviet Union until 1991
- Russian Federation
- Constituent republic within Russian Federation
- Member state (with Russian Federation) of CIS
- State not member of Commonwealth of Independent States
- ✹ Area of armed conflict
- Ethnic Russian immigrants
- Other refugees or returnees
- "Volga Germans" emigrating to Germany
- Asian immigrants

CHUKCHI

KORYAK

Petropavlovsk-Kamchatskiy

Yuzhno-Sakhalinsk

Magadan

Gizhiga

Okhotsk

Khabarovsk

Komsomolsk

BIROBIDZHAN

Verkhoyansk

Blagoveshchensk

SAKHA

Yakutsk

Chita

AGAY

BURYATIA

BURYATIA

Ulan Ude

UST ORDA
BURYATIA

Bratsk

Irkutsk

Khatanga

MONGOLIA

TAYMYR

EVENK

RUSSIA

Krasnoyarsk

KHAKASSIA

Novokuznetsk

TUVA

GORNO-
ALTAY

CHINA

Norilsk

Tomsk

Novosibirsk

Omsk

NENETS

Salekhard

YAMAL-
NENETS

KHANTY-
MANSI

Pavlodar

Semey

Karaganda

KAZAKHSTAN

Vorkuta

KOMI

Almo Ata

Bishkek

KYRGYZSTAN

TAJIKISTAN

KOMI-
PERMYAK

Yekaterinburg

Perm

UDMURTIA

Chelyabinsk

Ufa

BASHKORTOSTAN

Toshkent

Samarqand

UZBEKISTAN

Dushanbe

AFGHANISTAN

PAKISTAN

Murmansk

Arkhangelsk

KARELIA

St Petersburg

MARI EL

Kazan

TATARSTAN

Samara

Nizhniy
Novgorod

CHUVASHIA

MORDVINIA

Moscow

Volgograd

KALMYKIA

Astrakhan

Ashkhabad

TURKMENISTAN

IRAN

Tallinn

ESTONIA

Riga

LATVIA

Vilnius

Minsk

Kaliningrad
(Russia)

LITHUANIA

BELARUS

Kiev

UKRAINE

Rostov

Black
Sea

CRIMEA

DNESTR
REPUBLIC

MOLDOVA

GEORGIA

Map 2

ARMENIA

AZER-
BAIJAN

62. European Economic Integration since 1945

✳ ✳ ✳

The European Economic Community (EEC) was set up by the Treaty of Rome in 1957 and was renamed the European Community (EC) in 1967. As a first step toward stabilizing European currencies, the European Monetary System came into force in 1979. The Treaty on European Union was signed at Maastricht in February 7, 1992, and the single European currency system (euro) was launched on January 1, 1999.

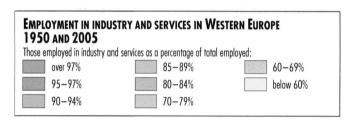

EMPLOYMENT IN INDUSTRY AND SERVICES IN WESTERN EUROPE 1950 AND 2005

Those employed in industry and services as a percentage of total employed:

over 97%	85–89%	60–69%
95–97%	80–84%	below 60%
90–94%	70–79%	

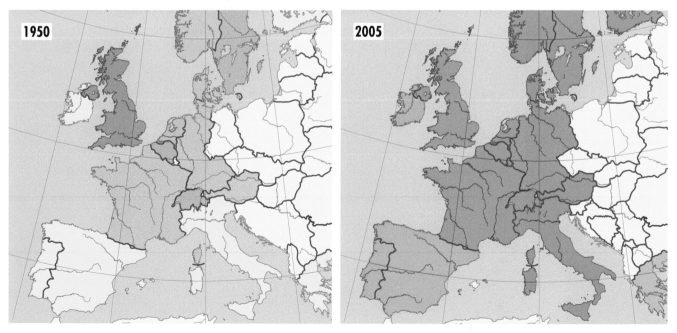

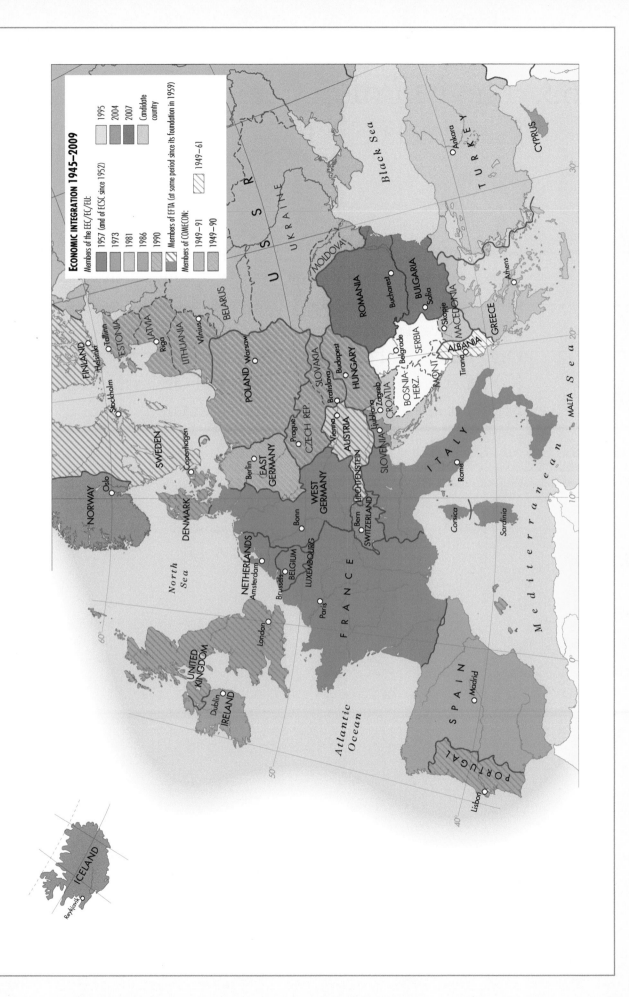

ECONOMIC INTEGRATION 1945–2009

Members of the EEC/EC/EU:
- 1957 (and of ECSC since 1952)
- 1973
- 1981
- 1986
- 1990
- 1995
- 2004
- 2007
- Candidate country

Members of EFTA (at some period since its foundation in 1959)

Members of COMECON:
- 1949–61
- 1949–91
- 1949–90

63. The Middle East and the Caucasus

✳ ✳ ✳

An estimated 70 percent of the world's known oil reserves are located in the Middle East and North Africa, mainly on the Arabian Peninsula and in the Gulf. The resultant oil boom facilitated the rapid modernization of the producer states. The Organization of Petroleum Exporting Countries (OPEC), whose most powerful members are in the Middle East, attempts to ensure a minimum price for crude oil by controlling supplies.

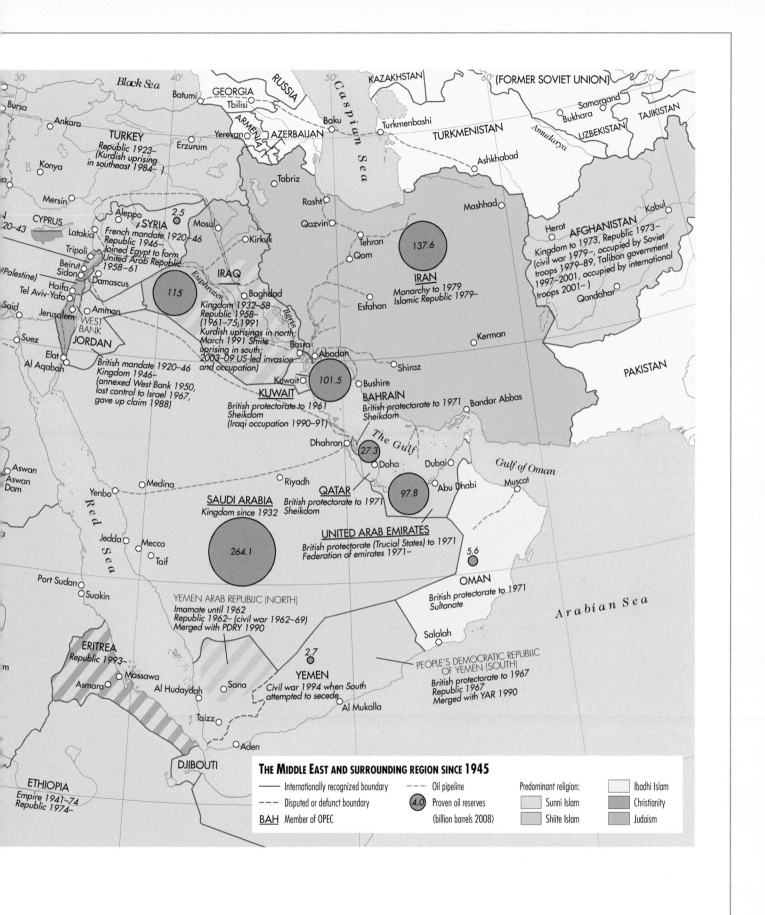

The following labels and text appear on the map:

Black Sea

Bursa
Ankara
Konya
Mersin
CYPRUS
20–43

Batumi
GEORGIA
Tbilisi
ARMENIA
Yerevan
AZERBAIJAN
Baku

RUSSIA

Caspian Sea

KAZAKHSTAN

(FORMER SOVIET UNION)

Samarqand
Bukhara
Turkmenbashi
TURKMENISTAN
Ashkhabad
Amudarya
UZBEKISTAN
TAJIKISTAN

TURKEY
Republic 1923–
(Kurdish uprising
in southeast 1984–)
Erzurum
Tabriz
Rasht
Qazvin
Mashhad
Kabul
Herat
AFGHANISTAN
Kingdom to 1973, Republic 1973–
(civil war 1979–, occupied by Soviet
troops 1979–89, Taliban government
1997–2001, occupied by international
troops 2001–)
Qandahar

Aleppo
2.5
Mosul
SYRIA
French mandate 1920–46
Republic 1946–
Joined Egypt to form
United Arab Republic
1958–61
Latakia
Tripoli
Beirut
Sidon
(Palestine)
Haifa
Tel Aviv-Yafo
Damascus
Euphrates
IRAQ
Kirkuk
Baghdad
115
Kingdom 1932–58
Republic 1958–
(1961–75; 1991
Kurdish uprisings in north;
March 1991 Shiite
uprising in south;
2003–09 US-led invasion
and occupation)
Tigris
Basra
Tehran
Qom
Esfahan
137.6
IRAN
Monarchy to 1979
Islamic Republic 1979–
Kerman
PAKISTAN

Said
Suez
Jerusalem
WEST
BANK
Amman
JORDAN
British mandate 1920–46
Kingdom 1946–
(annexed West Bank 1950,
lost control to Israel 1967,
gave up claim 1988)
Elat
Al Aqaba
Abadan
Kuwait
KUWAIT
British protectorate to 1961
Sheikdom
(Iraqi occupation 1990–91)
Shiraz
Bushire
BAHRAIN
British protectorate to 1971
Sheikdom
101.5
Bandar Abbas

Aswan
Aswan
Dam
Dhahran
27.3
Doha
The Gulf
Dubai
Gulf of Oman
Muscat

Red Sea
Yenbo
Medina
Riyadh
QATAR
British protectorate to 1971
Sheikdom
97.8
Abu Dhabi
Jedda
Mecca
Taif
SAUDI ARABIA
Kingdom since 1932
264.1
UNITED ARAB EMIRATES
British protectorate (Trucial States) to 1971
Federation of emirates 1971–
5.6
OMAN
British protectorate to 1971
Sultanate

Port Sudan
Suakin
YEMEN ARAB REPUBLIC (NORTH)
Imamate until 1962
Republic 1962– (civil war 1962–69)
Merged with PDRY 1990
Salalah
Arabian Sea

ERITREA
Republic 1993–
Massawa
Asmara
Al Hudaydah
Sana
2.7
YEMEN
Civil war 1994 when South
attempted to secede
Taizz
Al Mukalla
PEOPLE'S DEMOCRATIC REPUBLIC
OF YEMEN (SOUTH)
British protectorate to 1967
Republic 1967
Merged with YAR 1990

Aden
DJIBOUTI
ETHIOPIA
Empire 1941–74
Republic 1974–

THE MIDDLE EAST AND SURROUNDING REGION SINCE 1945

— Internationally recognized boundary
--- Disputed or defunct boundary
BAH Member of OPEC

--- Oil pipeline
(4.0) Proven oil reserves
(billion barrels 2008)

Predominant religion:
Sunni Islam
Shiite Islam

Ibadhi Islam
Christianity
Judaism

63. The Middle East and the Caucasus

* * *

The UN's proposed division of Israel was abandoned after Israeli independence in May 1948. Israel also expanded its territory in 1967 and 1973, although the Sinai region was returned to Egypt in 1979.

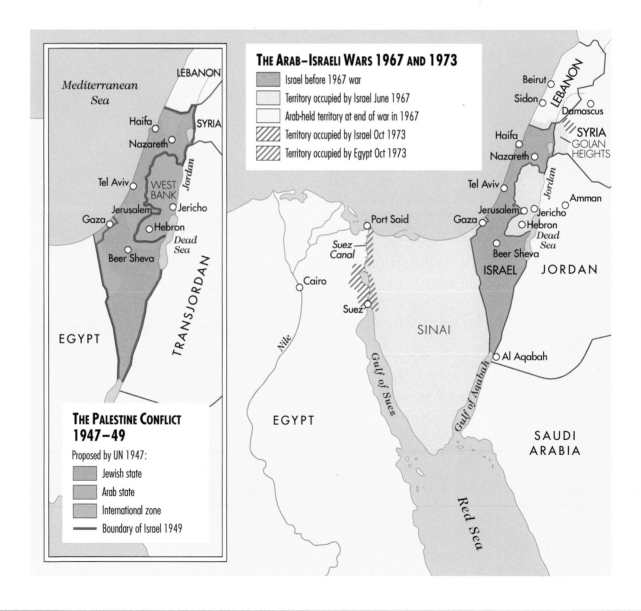

THE ARAB–ISRAELI WARS 1967 AND 1973

- Israel before 1967 war
- Territory occupied by Israel June 1967
- Arab-held territory at end of war in 1967
- Territory occupied by Israel Oct 1973
- Territory occupied by Egypt Oct 1973

THE PALESTINE CONFLICT 1947–49

Proposed by UN 1947:
- Jewish state
- Arab state
- International zone
- Boundary of Israel 1949

Ethnic tensions and summering rivalries in the Caucasus that were held in check by the Soviet Union broke out into armed conflicts after 1991. The most recent conflict was the brief but bloody Russo-Georgian War of 1998, instigated by the Russians to reassert control over the disputed region of South Ossetia.

CAUCASUS REGION 1988–2009

— International boundary

········· Boundary of constituent republic/autonomous region

Area ruled by Russian central government

Constituent republic within Russian Federation

Area that achieved *de facto* autonomy

✸ Area of armed conflict with date

64. War in the Balkans

1991–1999

* * *

In the constituent republics of the former Yugoslavia, democratically elected governments sought independence from the Serb-dominated Yugoslav Federation. The government of Serbia, however, was anxious to defend the rights of Serbs throughout the region, and bloody conflicts ensued. Despite the Dayton Peace Agreement of 1995, which divided Bosnia-Herzegovina into a Serb Republic and a Muslim/Croat Federation, in 1998 there were still around 1.5 million refugees and displaced persons in the region as a whole (and a further quarter of a million elsewhere in Europe). In 1999 the crisis in Kosovo led to another massive movement of people as more than 850,000 ethnic Albanian Kosovans fled from Yugoslavia.

The UN, which became involved in Bosnia in 1992, lacked sufficient military strength to implement its policy. In the summer of 1995 it was forced to withdraw from two of the areas, Zepa and Srebrnica, that it was supposed to protect, leaving them to be overrun by Bosnian Serbs.

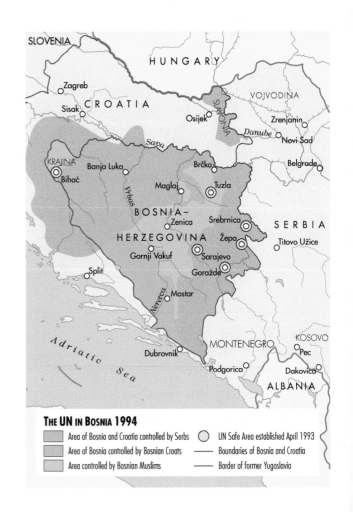

THE UN IN BOSNIA 1994

▧ Area of Bosnia and Croatia controlled by Serbs	◯ UN Safe Area established April 1993
▧ Area of Bosnia controlled by Bosnian Croats	— Boundaries of Bosnia and Croatia
▧ Area controlled by Bosnian Muslims	— Border of former Yugoslavia

AUSTRIA

HUNGARY

SLOVENIA

CROATIA

ROMANIA

23 ⬤81 274

SERB REPUBLIC OF
BOSNIA-HERZEGOVINA

11

110 ⬤49 110

105 ⬤117

FEDERATION
OF BOSNIA-
HERZEGOVINA

FEDERAL REPUBLIC
OF YUGOSLAVIA

105 206

110

SERBIA

105 20

15 MONTENEGRO

6

70

KOSOVO
⬤60?

BULGARIA

Adriatic Sea

ITALY

445 245

ALBANIA

FYR
MACEDONIA

GREECE

FORMER YUGOSLAVIA 1991–99

—— Boundary of former Yugoslavia 1991

—— Boundary established by Dayton Peace Agreement 1995

Croatia and Bosnia-Herzegovina (June 1998):

274 refugees (in thousands)

→ mainly Serb refugees

→ mainly Croat/Bosnian Muslim refugees

⬤49 displaced persons (in thousands)

Kosovo (mid-June 1999):

445 refugees (in thousands)

→ Ethnic Albanian refugees

⬤60? displaced persons (in thousands)

65. The United States as a Global Superpower

✳ ✳ ✳

As the United States became more powerful economically, it extended its area of involvement beyond the American continent to Africa, Southeast Asia, and Europe. Although it has sometimes considered it necessary to employ force to defend its interests, in many instances economic backing or, conversely, the threat of trade sanctions has been sufficient to achieve its objectives. ◆

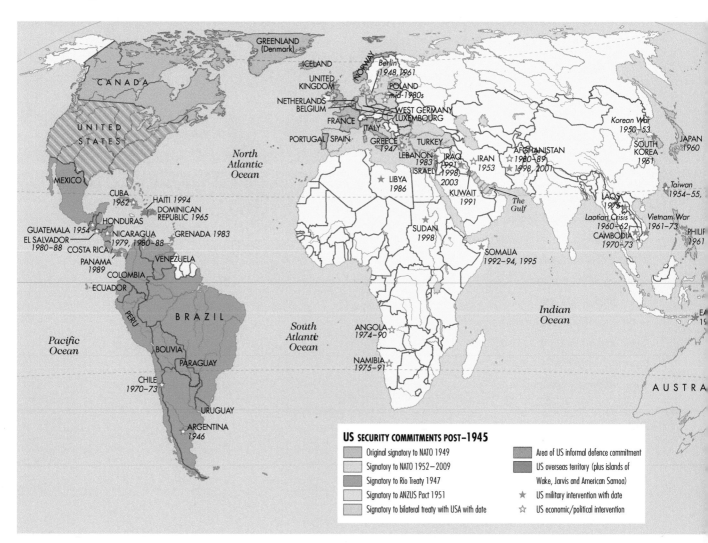

US SECURITY COMMITMENTS POST–1945

- Original signatory to NATO 1949
- Signatory to NATO 1952–2009
- Signatory to Rio Treaty 1947
- Signatory to ANZUS Pact 1951
- Signatory to bilateral treaty with USA with date
- Area of US informal defence commitment
- US overseas territory (plus islands of Wake, Jarvis and American Samoa)
- ★ US military intervention with date
- ☆ US economic/political intervention

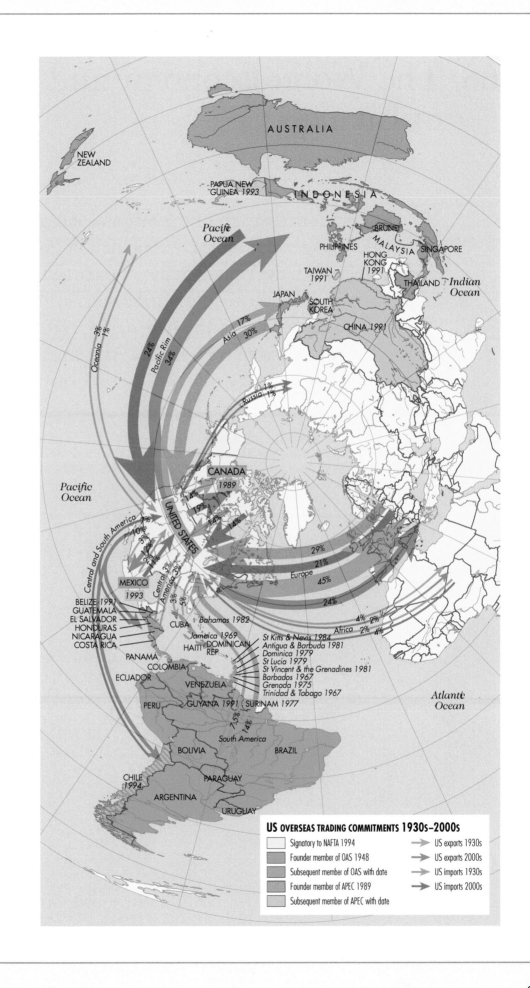

66. The World Economy and Standards of Living

✳ ✳ ✳

The comparative wealth of the major economies of the world changed during the second half of the 20th century. Although the United States maintained its position as the world's wealthiest nation, countries such as Argentina and Uruguay had slipped out of the "top 20" by 1970, while the newly industrialized countries of East Asia emerged as economic "tigers."

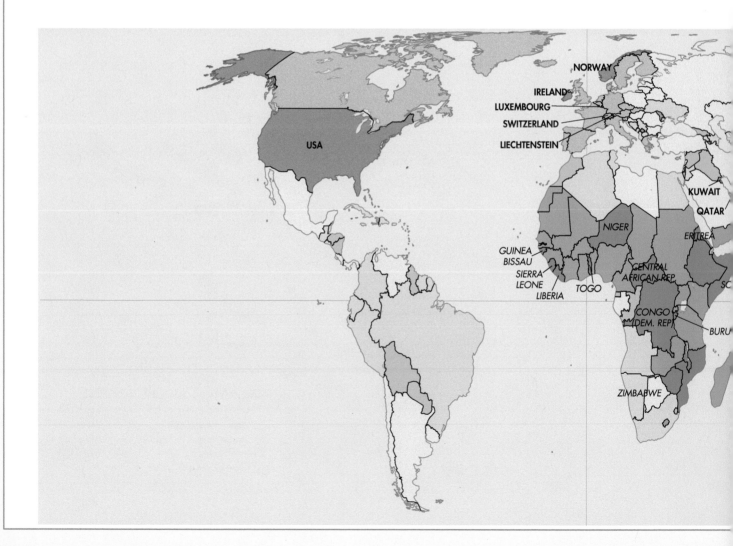

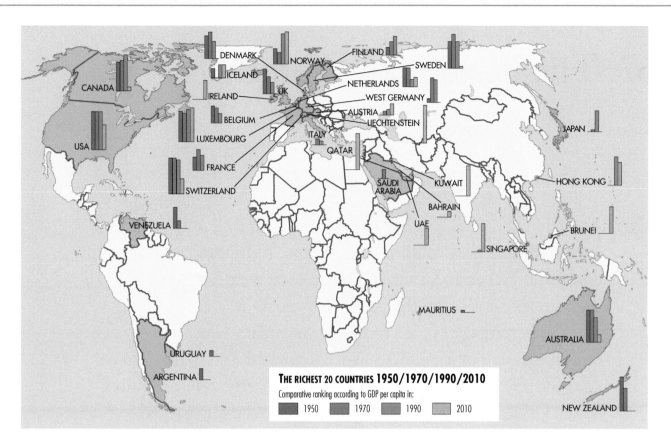

THE RICHEST 20 COUNTRIES 1950/1970/1990/2010

Comparative ranking according to GDP per capita in:

1950	1970	1990	2010

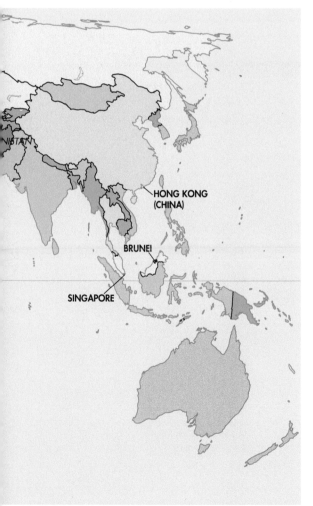

DISTRIBUTION OF WEALTH

A country's GDP per capita as percentage of world average ($10,500) 2009:

- over 400%
- 200–200%
- 100–200%
- 50–100%
- 25–50%
- 10–25%
- under 10%

LUX Country with GDP per capita among highest

MOZ Country with GDP per capita among lowest

The world's wealth is very unevenly distributed. The richest countries generate amounts of money that, when divided by the total population, produce (theoretical) per capita incomes over four times the world average; the equivalent figure for the poorest nations is one-tenth of the average.

67. The Position of Women

✳ ✳ ✳

While women in New Zealand were fully enfranchised as early as 1893, elsewhere in the world, with the exception of a few U.S. states, women had to wait until well into the 20th century before they could vote. In several European countries, including France and Switzerland, women were not given the right to vote until after the Second World War.

The percentage of girls receiving secondary education is a useful measure of a country's attitude toward its female citizens and the role they are expected to play in society. Some cultures still consider secondary education for girls a largely wasted investment.

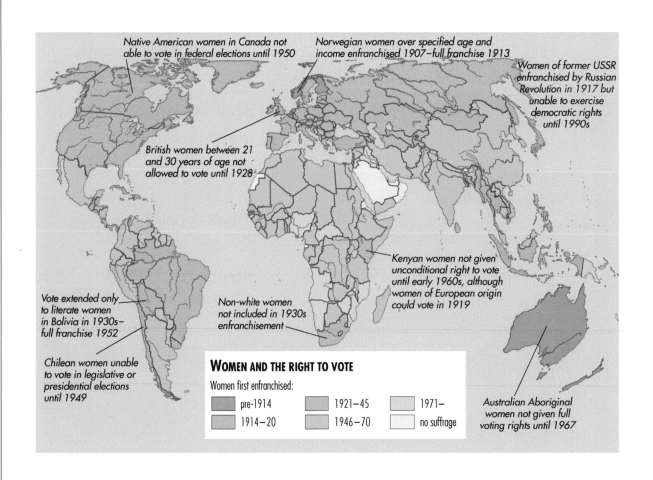

Native American women in Canada not able to vote in federal elections until 1950

Norwegian women over specified age and income enfranchised 1907–full franchise 1913

Women of former USSR enfranchised by Russian Revolution in 1917 but unable to exercise democratic rights until 1990s

British women between 21 and 30 years of age not allowed to vote until 1928

Kenyan women not given unconditional right to vote until early 1960s, although women of European origin could vote in 1919

Vote extended only to literate women in Bolivia in 1930s– full franchise 1952

Non-white women not included in 1930s enfranchisement

Chilean women unable to vote in legislative or presidential elections until 1949

Australian Aboriginal women not given full voting rights until 1967

WOMEN AND THE RIGHT TO VOTE

Women first enfranchised:

pre-1914	1921–45	1971–
1914–20	1946–70	no suffrage

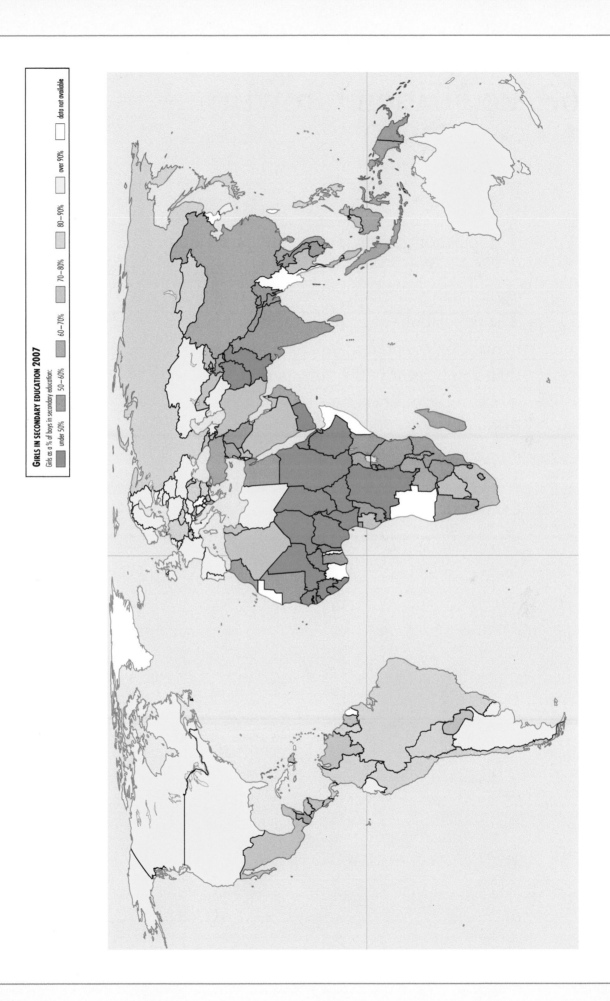

GIRLS IN SECONDARY EDUCATION 2007

Girls as a % of boys in secondary education:

- under 50%
- 50 – 60%
- 60 – 70%
- 70 – 80%
- 80 – 90%
- over 90%
- data not available

68. Population Growth since 1950

✳ ✳ ✳

Population growth is unevenly spread around the globe, with many more established industrial nations experiencing increases of less than 50 percent since 1950. The populations of many of the newly industrialized nations, on the other hand, have increased by more than 250 percent in the same period. Urbanization is one of the most extreme changes to have affected the world in the 20th century. In 1900 there were only a handful of cities with populations of over a million. By 2000 mega-cities were scattered around the world.

URBANIZATION OF THE WORLD

• City of at least 1 million inhabitants

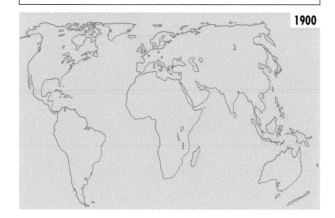

1900

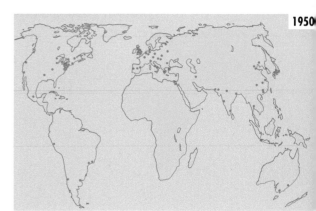

1950

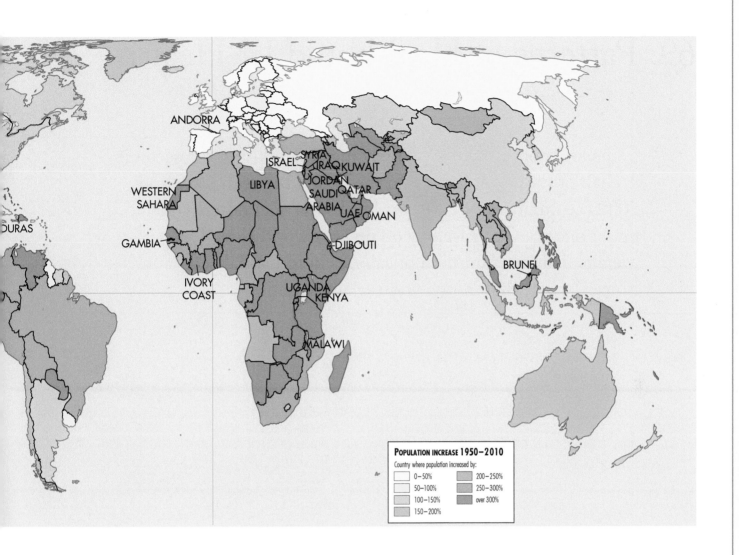

ANDORRA

ISRAEL SYRIA IRAQ KUWAIT
JORDAN
LIBYA SAUDI QATAR
WESTERN ARABIA
SAHARA UAE OMAN

GAMBIA DJIBOUTI

IVORY UGANDA
COAST KENYA

MALAWI

BRUNEI

DURAS

POPULATION INCREASE 1950–2010

Country where population increased by:

	0–50%		200–250%
	50–100%		250–300%
	100–150%		over 300%
	150–200%		

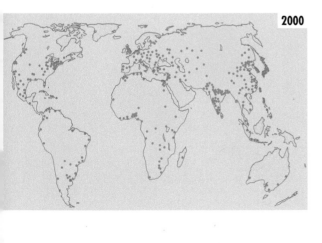

2000

69. Patterns of Health and Ill-Health

✳ ✳ ✳

S pending on health care largely increased during the second half of the 20th century. In the period between 1990 and 2009 the number of deaths per live births of children aged under one year decreased by 60 percent worldwide. The average daily consumption of calories in industrialized nations is nearly twice that in non-industrialized nations.

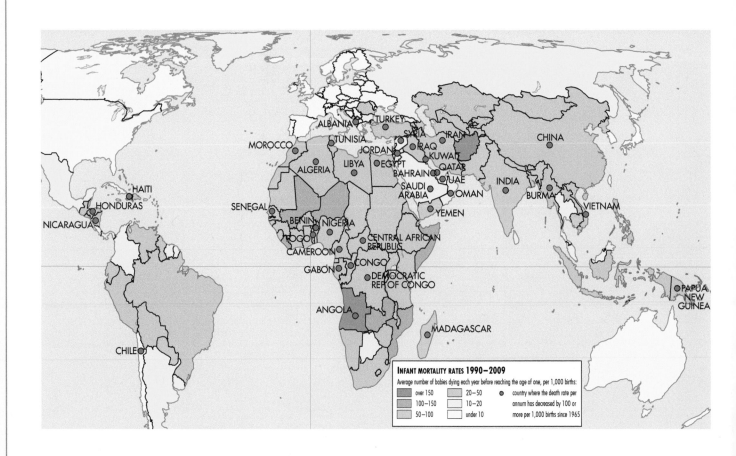

INFANT MORTALITY RATES 1990–2009

Average number of babies dying each year before reaching the age of one, per 1,000 births:

over 150	20–50	● country where the death rate per
100–150	10–20	annum has decreased by 100 or
50–100	under 10	more per 1,000 births since 1965

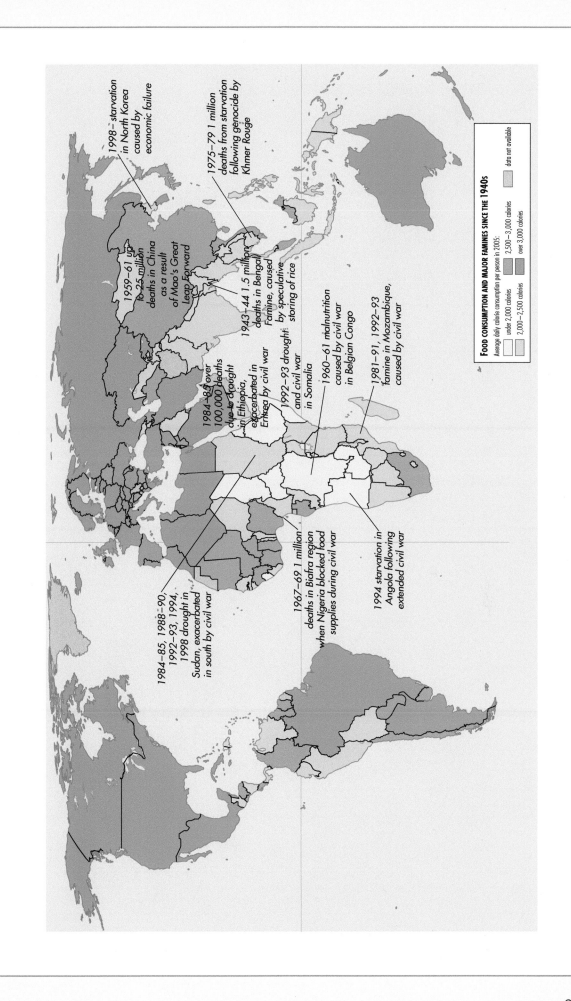

FOOD CONSUMPTION AND MAJOR FAMINES SINCE THE 1940s

Average daily calorie consumption per person in 2005:

- under 2,000 calories
- 2,000–2,500 calories
- 2,500–3,000 calories
- over 3,000 calories
- data not available

1998– starvation in North Korea caused by economic failure

1975–79 1 million deaths from starvation following genocide by Khmer Rouge

1959–61 up to 25 million deaths in China as a result of Mao's Great Leap Forward

1943–44 1.5 million deaths in Bengal Famine, caused by speculative storing of rice

1984–85 over 100,000 deaths due to drought in Ethiopia, exacerbated in Eritrea by civil war

1992–93 drought and civil war in Somalia

1960–61 malnutrition caused by civil war in Belgian Congo

1981–91, 1992–93 famine in Mozambique, caused by civil war

1984–85, 1988–90, 1992–93, 1994, 1998 drought in Sudan, exacerbated in south by civil war

1967–69 1 million deaths in Biafra region when Nigeria blocked food supplies during civil war

1994 starvation in Angola following extended civil war

69. Patterns of Health and Ill-Health

* * *

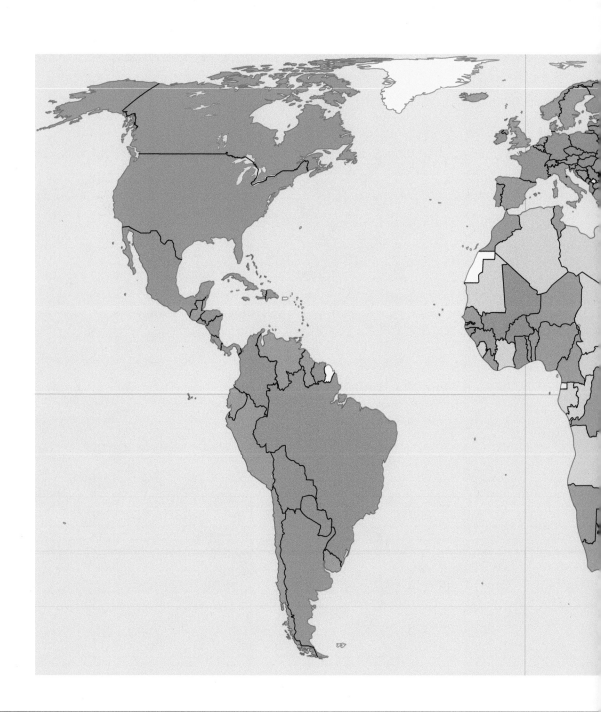

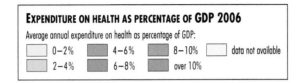

EXPENDITURE ON HEALTH AS PERCENTAGE OF GDP 2006

Average annual expenditure on health as percentage of GDP:

0−2%	4−6%	8−10%
2−4%	6−8%	over 10%

data not available

70. The Changing Environment

✳ ✳ ✳

The world's tropical rain forests are being cut down at an ever-increasing rate. The timber trade makes an important contribution to the economies of many tropical regions and population growth has also created demand for more farmland. Acid deposition is caused by high levels of sulfur and nitrogen being discharged into the atmosphere by industrial processes. Despite attempts by many governments to clean up the air in their cities, the increasing use of motorized transport has contributed to unacceptable levels of pollution in many of the world's cities.

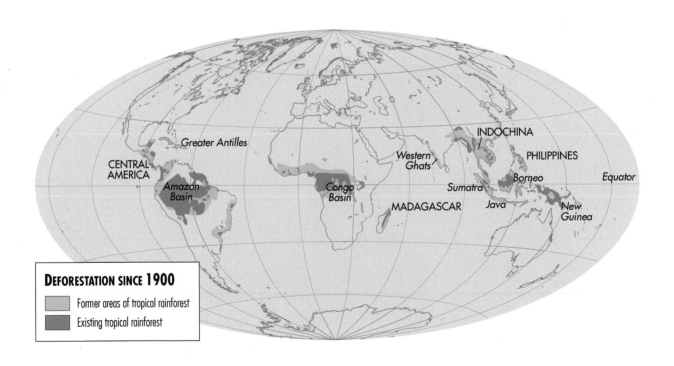

DEFORESTATION SINCE 1900
Former areas of tropical rainforest
Existing tropical rainforest

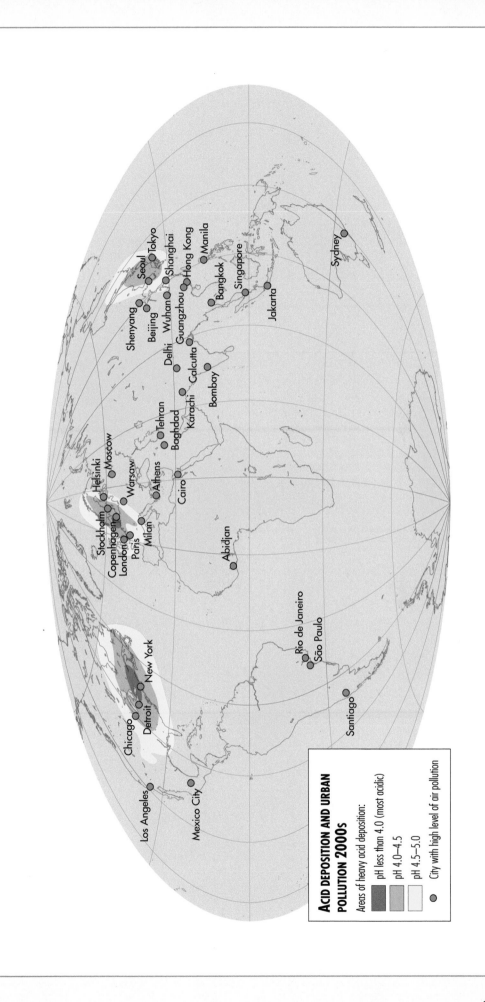

ACID DEPOSITION AND URBAN POLLUTION 2000s

Areas of heavy acid deposition:

pH less than 4.0 (most acidic)

pH 4.0–4.5

pH 4.5–5.0

City with high level of air pollution

Los Angeles
Mexico City
Chicago
Detroit
New York

Rio de Janeiro
São Paulo

Santiago

Stockholm
Copenhagen
London
Paris
Helsinki
Moscow
Warsaw
Milan
Athens

Tehran
Baghdad
Karachi
Bombay

Cairo

Abidjan

Shenyang
Beijing
Seoul
Tokyo
Wuhan
Shanghai
Hong Kong
Manila
Guangzhou
Delhi
Calcutta
Bangkok
Singapore
Jakarta

Sydney

101

Outline Maps

Renaissance Italy

✳ ✳ ✳

1. Identify and label these cities:
   a) Florence
   b) Siena
   c) Milan
   d) Venice
   e) Rome
   f) Genoa
   g) Naples
   h) Mantua
   i) Bologna
   j) Palermo

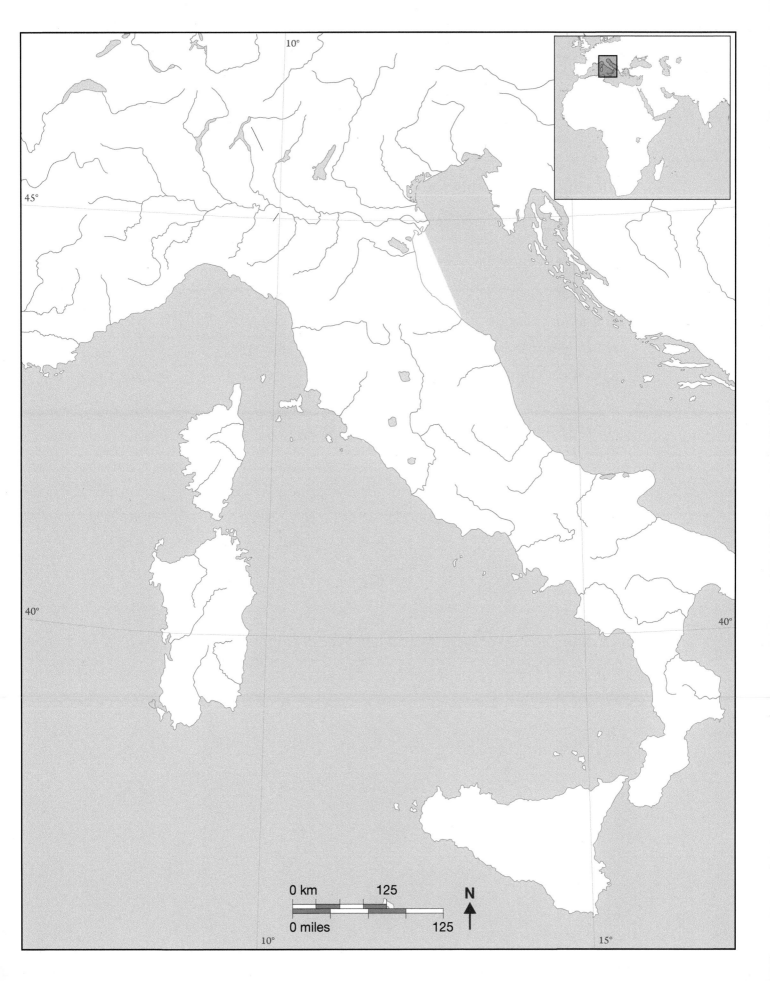

0 km   125

0 miles   125

N

Africa and the Mediterranean, 1497

✳ ✳ ✳

1. Identify and label these places:
   a) Morocco
   b) Mali
   c) Sahara
   d) Sahel
   e) Canary Islands
   f) Cape Verde Islands
   g) Cape of Good Hope

2. Identify and label these cities and settlements:
   a) Lisbon
   b) Seville
   c) Timbuktu
   d) São Jorge da Mina
   e) Mina
   f) Calicut

3. On the inset map, identify and label these empires:
   a) Aztec Empire
   b) Inca Empire

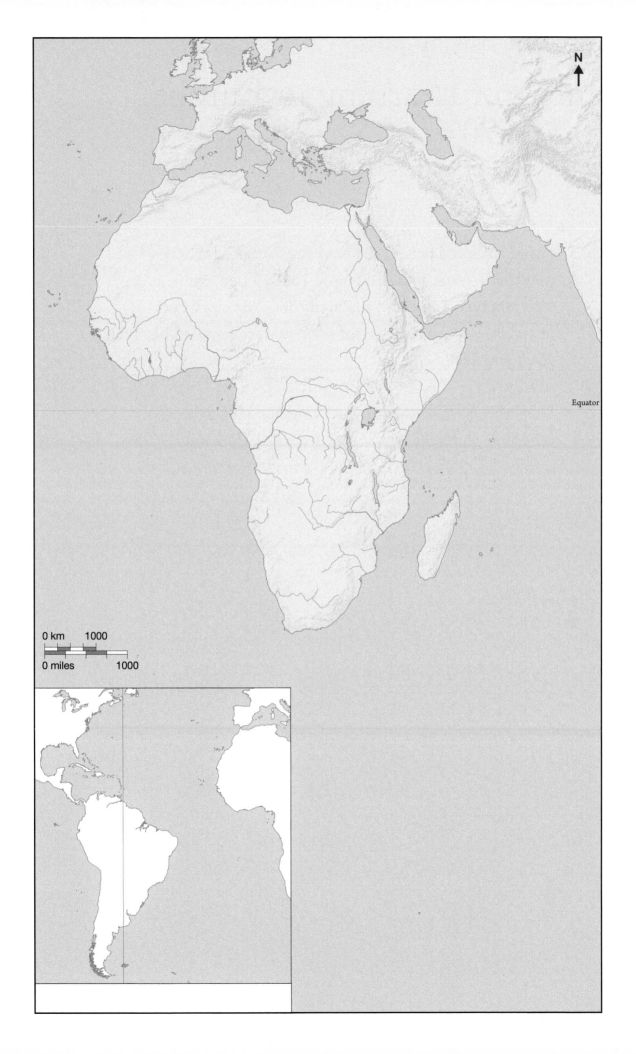

Equator

0 km   1000

0 miles   1000

N

Centers of Learning in Europe, 1500–1770

* * *

1. Using a colored pencil, shade in those regions where universities were founded before 1500. Then, using a different colored pencil, shade in those regions where universities and academies of science were founded between 1500 and 1770.

    Does this exercise suggest anything about social and economic shifts within Europe between 1500 and 1770?

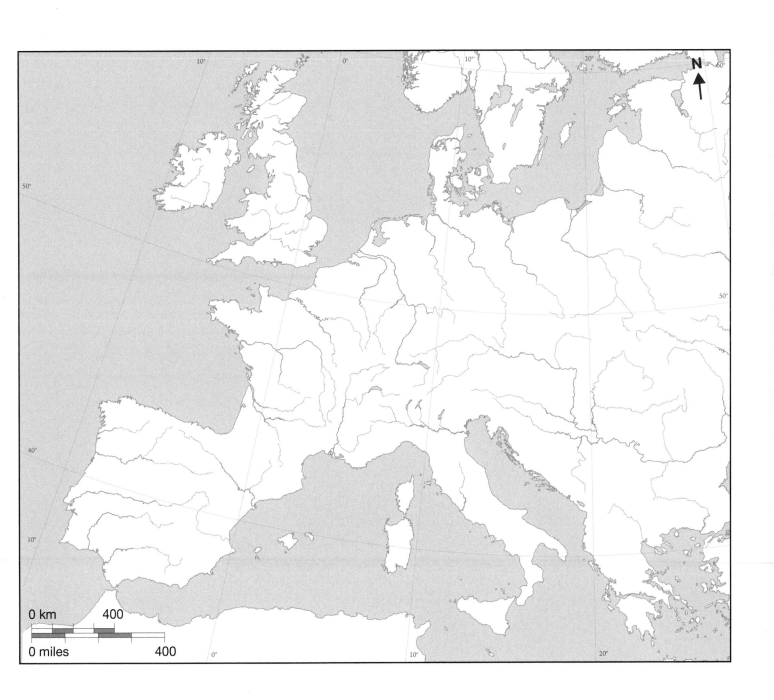

109

Europe in 1648

* * *

1. Identify and label these places:
   a) Spain
   b) Portugal
   c) Scotland, Ireland, England
   d) Denmark and Norway
   e) Sweden
   f) Poland-Lithuania
   g) Ottoman Empire
   h) Austria
   i) Hungary
   j) Papal States
   k) Switzerland
   l) Prussia
   m) Spanish Netherlands
   n) Holland

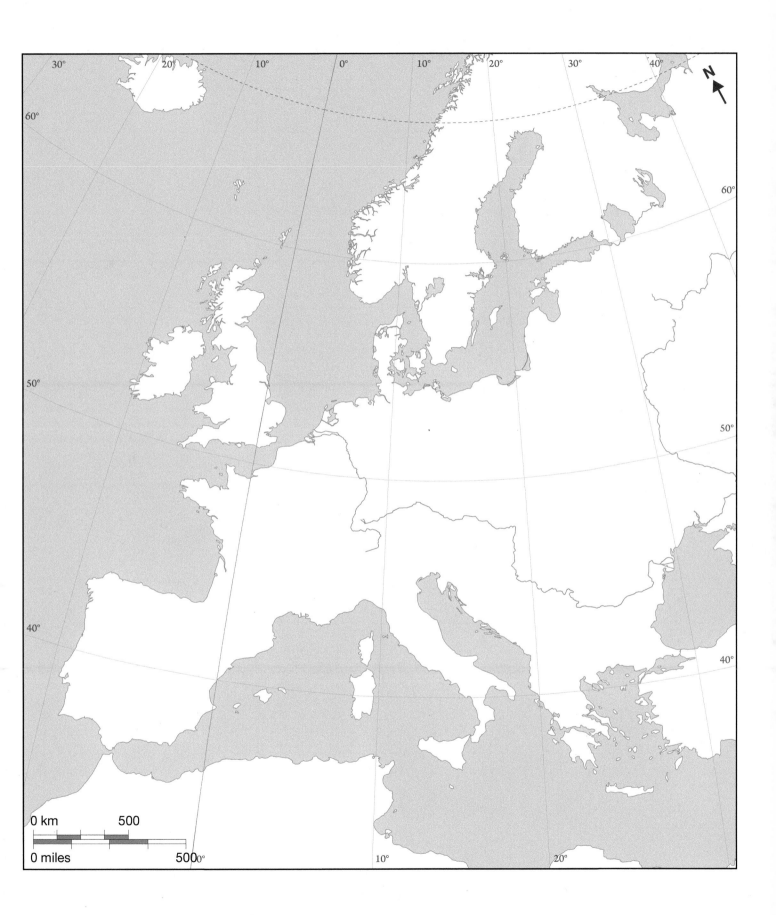

Subscriptions to the *Encyclopédie*

✳ ✳ ✳

1. Identify and label these cities:
    a) Paris
    b) London
    c) Madrid
    d) Barcelona
    e) Marseilles
    f) Turin
    g) Geneva
    h) Rouen
    i) Bordeaux
    j) Brussels
    k) Amsterdam
    l) Warsaw
    m) St. Petersburg

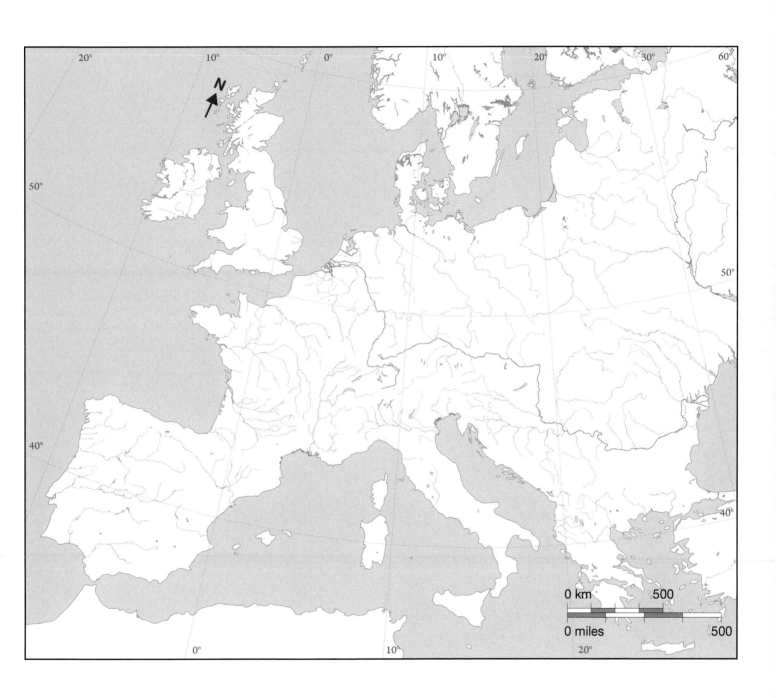

113

Napoleonic Europe, 1796–1815

✳ ✳ ✳

1. Shade those countries that were either under direct
   French control, ruled by Napoleon or members of his family,
   or dependencies of France.

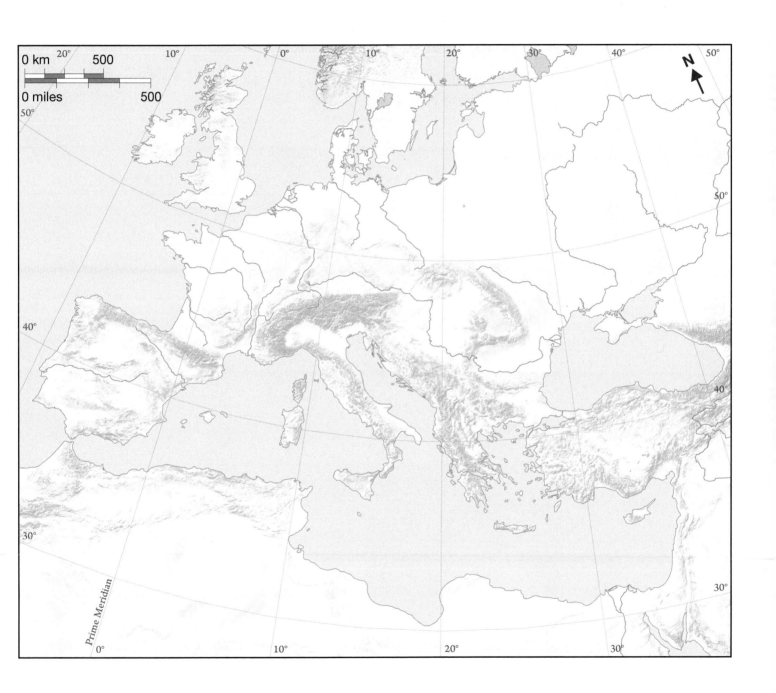

0 km 20° 500

0 miles 500

50°

40°

30°

Prime Meridian

0°

10°

20°

30°

50°

40°

30°

20°

10°

0°

10°

20°

30°

40°

50°

50°

50°

40°

30°

N

115

Industrializing Europe by 1871

* * *

1. Using a colored pencil, shade in those areas where coal mining predominated.
2. Identify and label these cities:
    a) Manchester
    b) Birmingham
    c) Newcastle
    d) Lille
    e) Cologne
    f) Frankfurt
    g) Antwerp

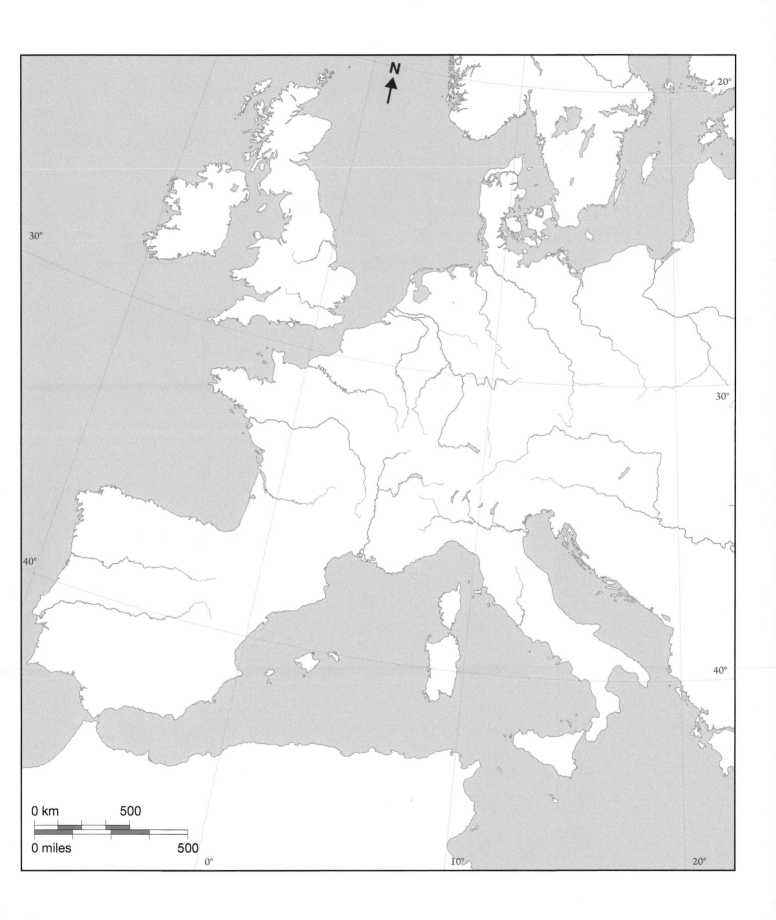

Centers of Revolution, 1848

✳ ✳ ✳

1. Identify and label these states:
   a) Austrian Empire
   b) Piedmont and Sardinia
   c) Kingdom of the Two Sicilies
   d) Belgium
   e) Luxembourg
   f) Prussia
   g) Greece
   h) Ottoman Empire
   i) Russia
   j) United Kingdom
   k) France

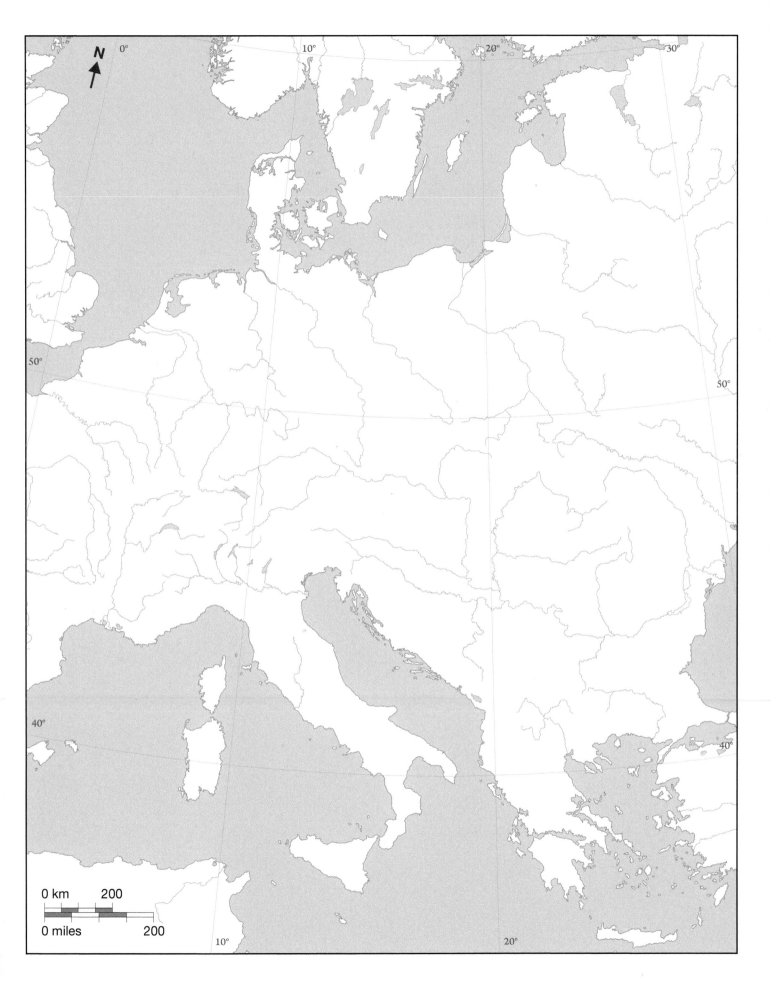

N

0°　　10°　　20°　　30°

50°　　　　　　　　　　　　　　50°

40°　　　　　　　　　　　　　　40°

0 km　　200

0 miles　　200

10°　　　　　　20°

The Peoples of the West, ca. 1850

* * *

1. On the main map, identify and label the homeland for each
   of these ethnic groups:
   a) Basques
   b) Welsh
   c) Walloons
   d) Flemish
   e) Normans
   f) Alsatians
   g) Catalans
   h) Finns
   i) Ukranians

2. On the inset map, use colored pencils to shade in those areas
   inhabited by each of these ethnic groups:
   a) Croats
   b) Serbs
   c) Hungarians
   d) Slovenes
   e) Czechs
   f) Germans
   g) Slovaks

121

Jewish Emigration from Russia, 1880–1914

∗ ∗ ∗

1. On the map, identify and label these cities:
   a) Vienna
   b) Leipzig
   c) Berlin
   d) Warsaw
   e) Paris
   f) Montpelier
   g) Marseilles
   h) Geneva
   i) Zurich

2. Identify and label these rivers:
   a) Danube
   b) Dniester
   c) Dnieper
   d) Oder
   e) Elbe
   f) Rhine
   g) Seine
   h) Loire
   i) Rhône
   j) Ebro

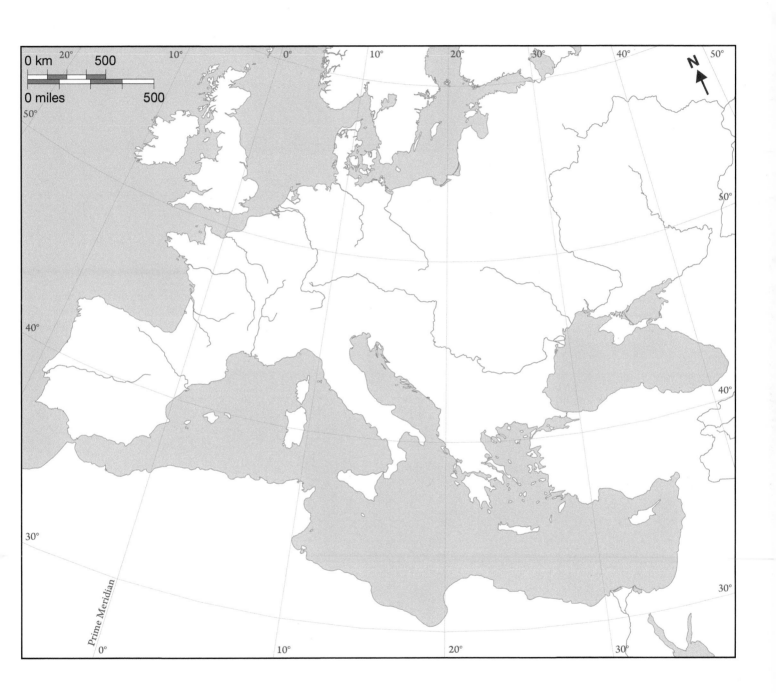

0 km   20°   500

0 miles   500

50°

40°

30°

Prime Meridian

0°

10°

20°

30°

40°

50°

N

Winning the Vote: Women's Suffrage in the Greater West, 1906–1971

* * *

1. Which regions of the Greater West were the first to extend suffrage to women?

2. Review pages 792-796 of The Cultures of the West. Ultimately, what were the reasons why some countries granted women the right to vote earlier than other countries?

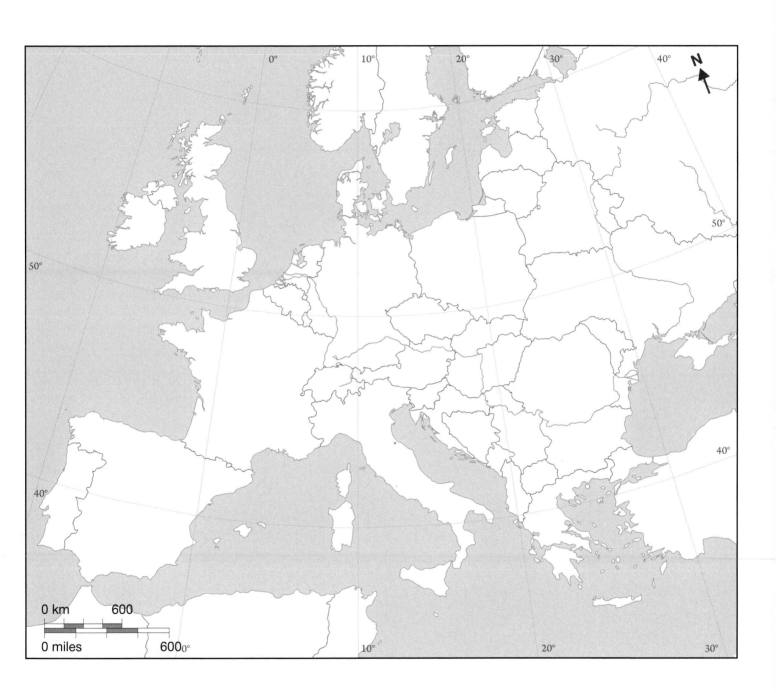

The Scramble for Africa

✳ ✳ ✳

1. Using a colored pencil, shade in those regions colonized by these European powers:
   a) Britain
   b) France
   c) Belgium
   d) Germany
   e) Italy
   f) Portugal
   g) Spain

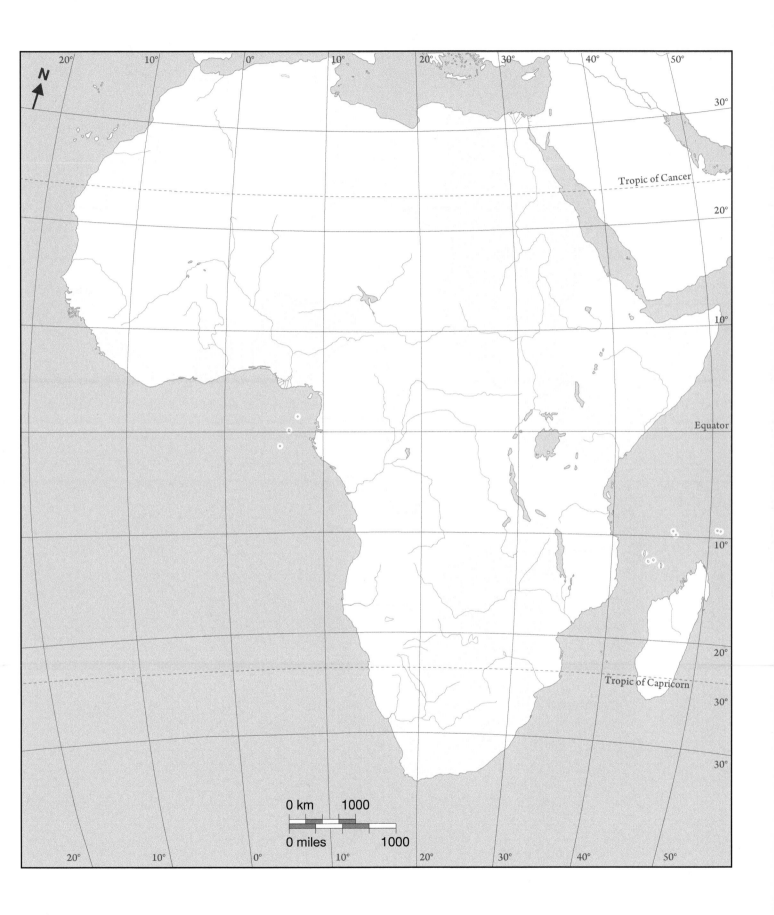

20°   10°   0°   10°   20°   30°   40°   50°

N

30°

Tropic of Cancer

20°

10°

Equator

10°

20°

Tropic of Capricorn

30°

30°

0 km   1000

0 miles   1000

20°   10°   0°   10°   20°   30°   40°   50°

Europe and the Middle East in 1914 and 1923

* * *

Identify and label these empires:
   a) Austria-Hungary
   b) Russian Empire
   c) Ottoman Empire

Identify and label these countries and mandates:
   a) Czechoslovakia
   b) Yugoslavia
   c) Soviet Union
   d) Austria
   e) Hungary
   f) Turkey
   g) Syria
   h) Iraq
   i) Transjordan
   j) Palestine
   k) Lithuania
   l) Latvia
   m) Estonia
   n) Poland

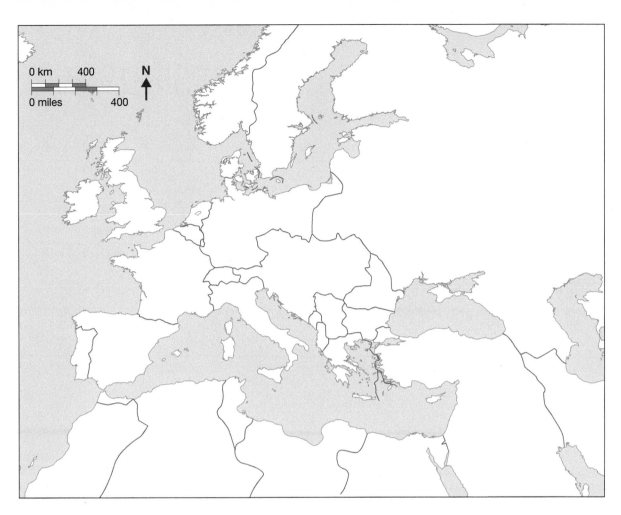

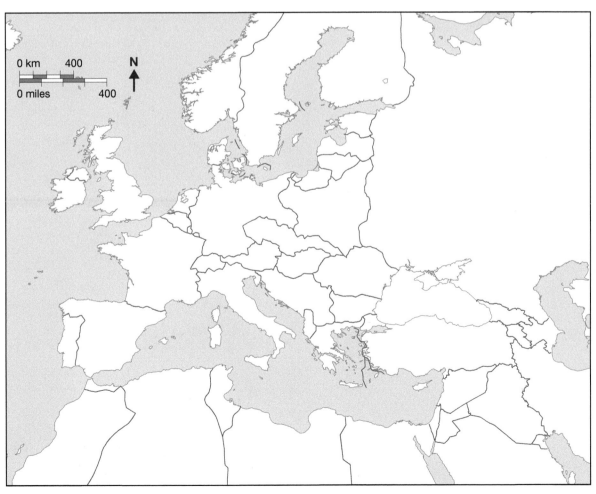

World War II in Europe, 1939–1945

* * *

1. Shade in the maximum extent of territory under Axis control by November 1942.

2. Using colored pencils, draw lines to show the Western Allied advance by May 1945 and the Soviet advance by December 1944.

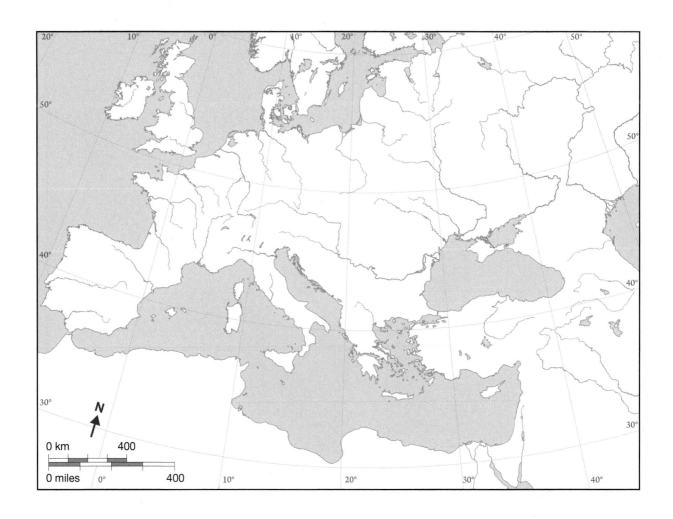

World War II in the Pacific, 1937–1945

✳ ✳ ✳

1. Draw a circle to show the furthest line of Japanese advance, July 1942.

2. Identify and label these places:
   a) Hawaii   f) Okinawa
   b) Midway   g) Hiroshima
   c) New Guinea   h) Nagasaki
   d) Philippines   i) Nanjing
   e) Iwo Jima   j) Tokyo

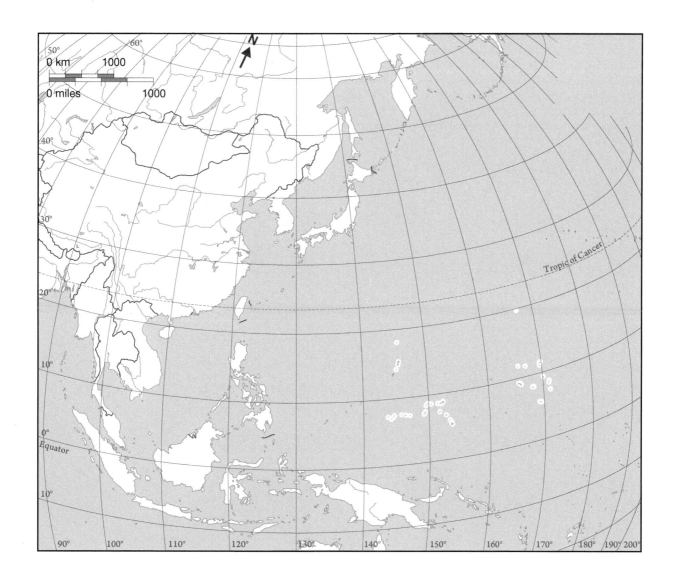

Military Blocs in Europe, 1948–1955

* * *

1. Draw a line that shows the "Iron Curtain" dividing Europe in half.

2. Using colored pencils, shade in those countries that were members of NATO and the Warsaw Pact in 1955.

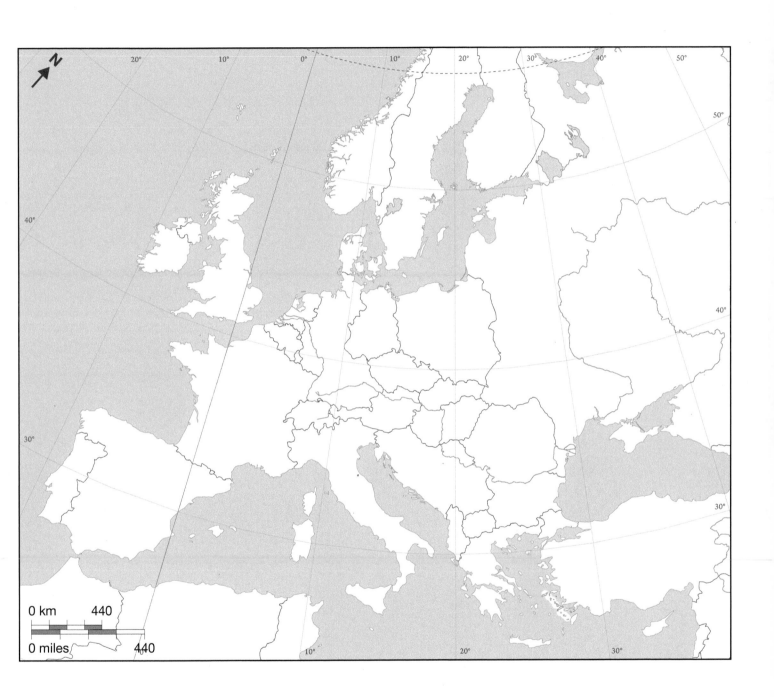

0 km 440

0 miles 440

Jewish Immigration to Israel, 1948–2012

* * *

1. Identify and label Israel

2. Identify and label these countries from which many Jews emigrated between 1948 and 2012:
   a) Soviet Union
   b) Poland
   c) Hungary
   d) Czechoslovakia
   e) Romania
   f) France
   g) Morocco
   h) Algeria
   i) Tunisia
   j) Libya
   k) Egypt
   l) Germany
   m) Yugoslavia
   n) Turkey
   o) Iraq
   p) Iran
   q) Greece
   r) Syria

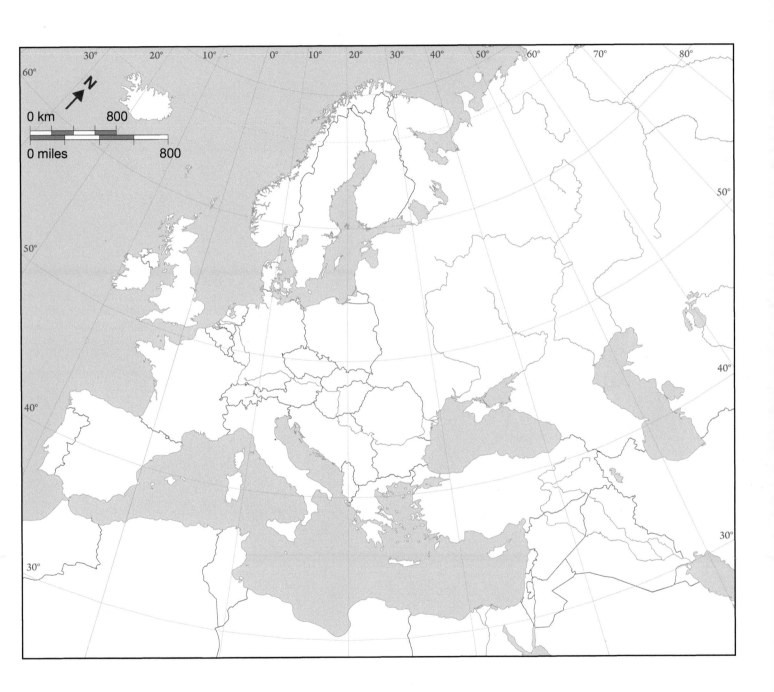

135

The Fall of Communism in Eastern Europe and the Soviet Union

* * *

1. Using a colored pencil, shade those former Soviet republics that gained independence in 1991.

2. Using a colored pencil, shade those former Warsaw Pact countries that held free elections in 1990–1992.

3. Identify and label these countries and regions:
   a) Georgia
   b) Armenia
   c) Azerbaijan
   d) Chechnya
   e) Uzbekistan
   f) Turkmenistan
   g) Kirghizstan
   h) Tajikistan
   i) Kazakhstan
   j) Latvia
   k) Estonia

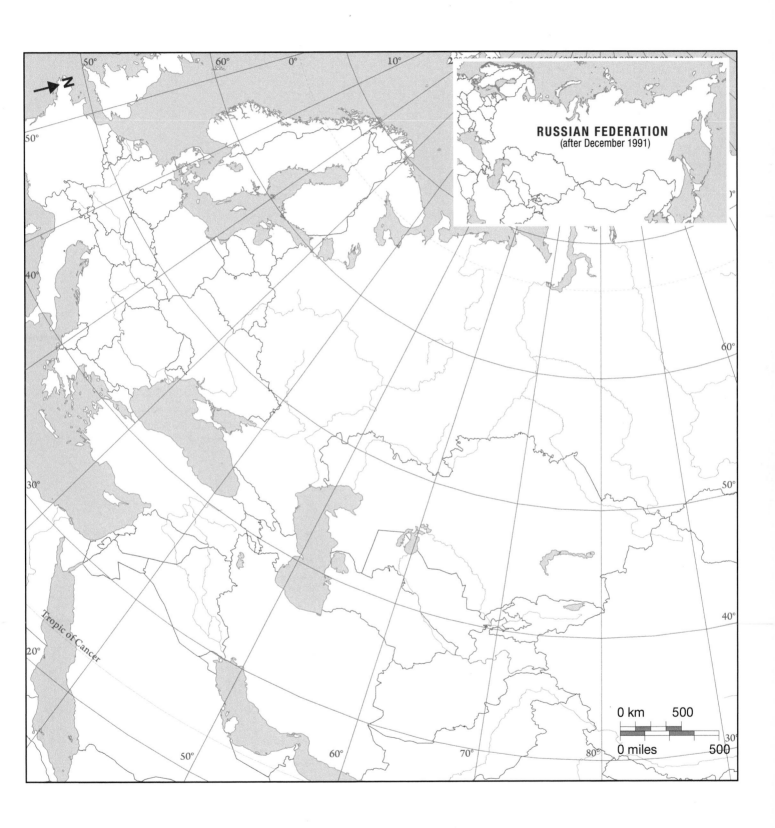

RUSSIAN FEDERATION
(after December 1991)

0 km   500

0 miles   500

Tropic of Cancer

Wars and Conflicts in the Greater West, 1990–2012

✳ ✳ ✳

1. Identify and label these areas of conflict in the Greater West:
   a) Former Yugoslavia
   b) Transnistria
   c) Abkhazia
   d) South Ossetia
   e) Chechnya
   f) Nagorno-Karabakh
   g) Israel/Gaza
   h) Lebanon
   i) Libya
   j) Syria
   k) Yemen
   l) Gulf region (Iraq, Kuwait, Iran)
   m) Afghanistan

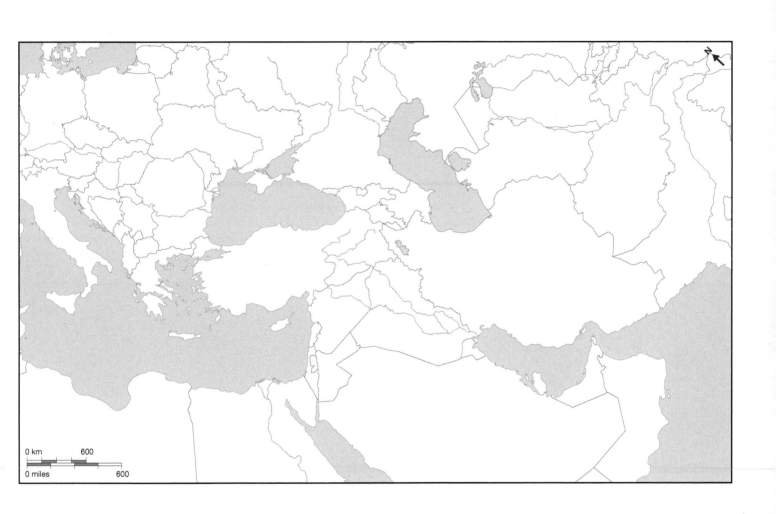